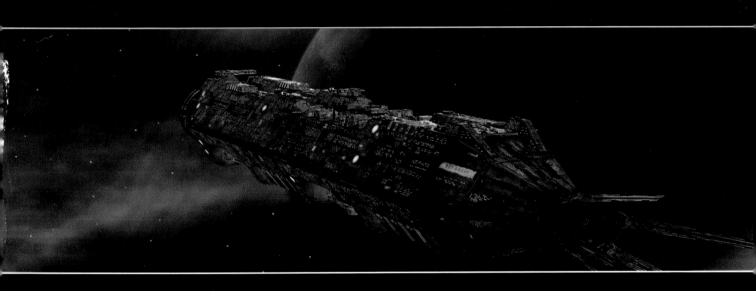

may the farce be with you...

First published in Great Britain in 1999 by Virgin Publishing Ltd

This edition produced for
The Book People Ltd,
Hall Wood Avenue,
Haydock,
St Helens WA11 9UL

A catalogue record of this book is available from the British Library.

ISBN 185613-636-1

Printed in Belgium

Colour Origination by Colourwise Ltd

Designed by Andy Spence

# RED DWARF™ VIII

FOREWORD & EPISODE INTRODUCTIONS BY
**DOUG NAYLOR**

**TED SMART**

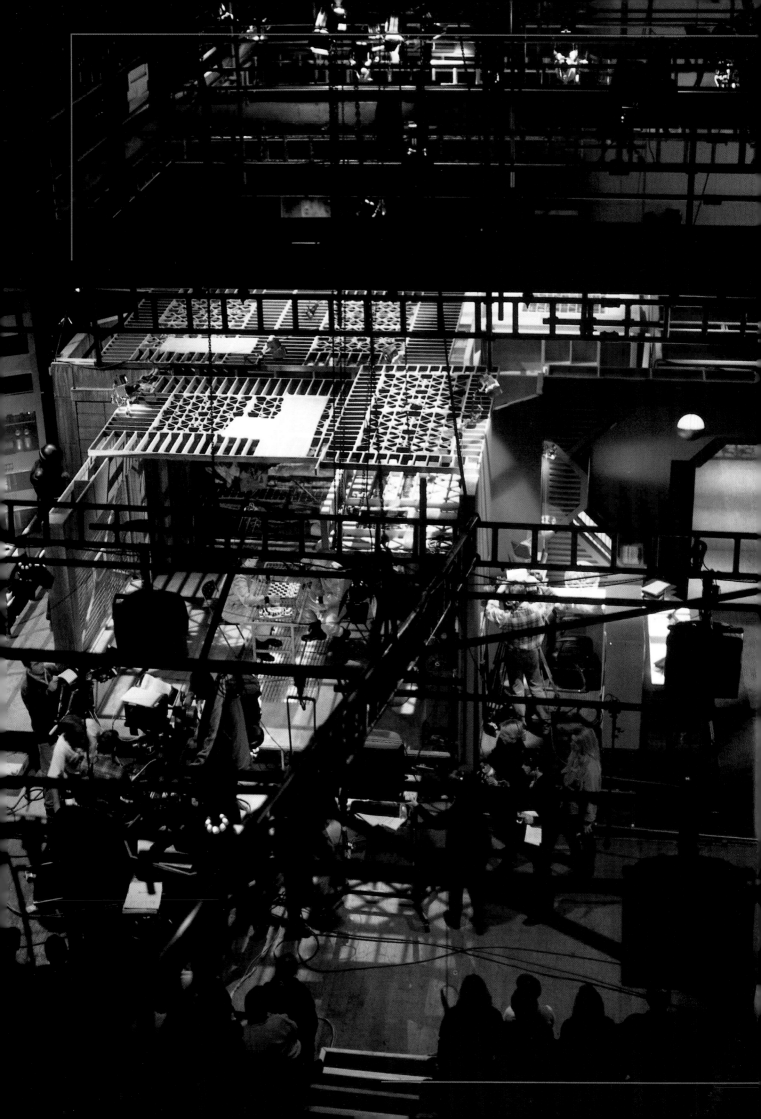

# CONTENTS

# FOREWORD
BY DOUG NAYLOR.

I awoke suddenly and sat bolt upright in bed, my heart thumping like the bass speaker in a drug dealer's Capri. The room was shrouded in a luxuriant thick blackness, a black that was so black, it could have won awards for its blackness. My eyesight adjusted and the gloom gave way to various strange shapes: a chair, a desk, a pamphlet listing tourist attractions in the Shepperton/Staines area.

Where was I?

A half-drunk pint of Boddingtons stood on the bed-side table.

My skin was Saharan dry and I had a bogey in my left nostril that was so hard you could have banged it into a wall and hung up a picture. Only one thing does that to bogeys - hotel air-conditioning systems.

My brain slowly began to splutter into life. We were editing Red Dwarf VII. That night, like the previous three nights, we'd finished at three in the morning and were due to start again at nine thirty. I'd decided to avoid the three-hour round trip home. Hence the hotel.

Then I realized what had woken me.

My hand dived under the covers and I felt something wet. I held it up for inspection in the gloom. It was warm and appeared to be dark in colour.

Blood.

Lots of blood.

Lots of *my* blood.

And not my favourite place for my blood, which has always been inside my body. This was outside and lots and lots of it. My entire lower body. I was soaked in the stuff.

I'd been knifed while I slept.

But who would knife me?

Quickly, I started to compile a list - it included every editor I'd ever worked with for driving them nuts asking them to constantly re-edit the show, every sound engineer I'd ever worked with for driving them nuts for constantly - to cut a long list short, when I passed twenty I stopped, realizing this could take several hours and decided I had to deal with the matter in hand.

I stretched out and tremulously clicked on the hotel table light.

I was going to look like that guy in *Reservoir Dogs*. I just knew it.

I braced myself for a shock but, even so, what I saw appalled me.

It wasn't blood.

It was something much much worse.

A warm brown substance covered my stomach, upper thighs and buttocks. I gagged in self-disgust. This is what making Red Dwarf can do to you, I thought. I've lost control of my bodily functions. They'll have to put me in a home with little old ladies who play carpet bowls all day and read *What Zimmer.*

But something was wrong - the brown stuff: it smelt minty.

Gingerly, I tasted it.

I'm sorry if that appals you, but that's what I did - this is a true story. And when I tasted it I didn't expect it'd ever appear in the introduction of any book, so I thought I was pretty safe in tasting it, in that no-one would ever find out.

But that's what I did - I tasted it.

Not only did it smell minty, it tasted minty.

And then I realised - I'd fallen asleep on one of the hotel's complimentary mints. The ones they sometimes leave on the sheets when they turn the down the bed.

Why they leave chocolates on your sheets, God only knows. Who needs a chocolate covered mint just before they go to sleep?

OK, Dawn French.

But apart from Dawn French who else? And how come all hotels put them out on the off-chance Dawn's staying?

I gazed at the sheets.

What was the maid going to think when she entered my room, in that split second before she worked out some idiot had slept on one of her mints.

I sat up, grabbed my underpants, dipped them into the glass of Boddingtons and started to clean up the chocolate as best I could.

Yes, OK, in retrospect this wasn't very smart. But I'd been surviving on about four hours sleep for the past week, plus I'd just woken up and my brain wasn't working, double plus I'm extremely stupid anyway.

I looked at the mess I was making.

I was making it worse.

Boddingtons doesn't remove complimentary mints from bed sheets - take my word for it.

Now the mixture had gone through the sheets and down into the mattress.

I got out of bed and dashed into the gloom of the bathroom. Some disgusting slob had left a half-eaten burger which they'd half scoffed while they soaked in the bath the night before. It sat there, by the wash basin, next to the basket of shampoo sachets. I grabbed one and returned to the scene of the crime.

Shampoo, that would help.

I bit open the packet and poured it on.

Red shampoo.

Weird.

I rubbed it in.

Red shampoo - I'd never come across red shampoo. God, how pretentious, red bloody shampoo and even worse it smelt of tomato ketchup.

I'd grabbed a sachet of burger ketchup!

Now my bed sheet was covered in chocolate, beer and tomato sauce.

I got dressed, turned the mattress over and hurriedly put the sheets into a laundry bag, and at five o'clock in the morning found myself in an all-night laundry, watching my sheets slowly getting clean.

Such a small thing as a complimentary mint and yet it had caused such chaos.

Small things can cause chaos.

I started thinking. Thinking about Red Dwarf VIII.

Thinking about what would happen if the Nanobots revived the original crew then disappeared.

As I sat there I had the tiniest of tiny ideas that would eventually form the basis for the first episode of Series VIII.

Consequently, this book is dedicated to that complimentary mint.

If that little square of chocolate hadn't died so hideously, hurling itself at my hot, snoring body, then I wouldn't have wound up in an all-night laundry thinking about how small things can cause chaos.

It will always share a place in my heart, my torso and certain parts of my buttocks.

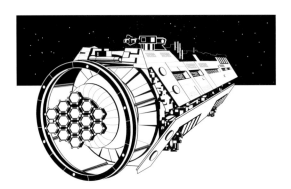

The sixth season and final series of Red Dwarf finished on the 11 of November 1993. A lot of the press and most of the fans appeared to hate it, saying it had become formulaic, retreading old ground and longed for the early series, especially II and III when they believed it had been at its peak.

Shortly afterwards Chris Barrie decided he no longer wanted to be involved in any further series; Rob Grant moved on to pastures new; Craig Charles wrongfully went to prison; Robert Llewellyn started writing novels; Norman Lovett had quit several years before and had gone to live in Edinburgh; Director, Ed Bye, had also dropped out after series IV to direct his wife Ruby Wax's new series and Danny John-Jules was busy working in the theatre. Even the six-foot, Red Dwarf, model ship wasn't available - it had fallen off a shelf at the BBC some years earlier and had been chucked into a skip.

I sat at my desk working on a new project, a movie, called rather unimaginatively at this stage: 'New Project', when the telephone rang. It was my agent, Charles, informing me, we were still contracted to the BBC to make two more series of Red Dwarf and as the only remaining creative director of Grant Naylor Productions I was legally bound to deliver.

'But Rob's left', I whined. 'And I want to do something new. Plus we've got no director, half the cast are unavailable or unwilling, there're no scripts and anyway I want to do something new. And did I mention I want to do something new?'

There was a pause before he replied. 'Red Dwarf VII has never been done before. That'd be new,' he said. 'And Red Dwarf VIII, well, that's entirely new too. Two new projects full of newness. And once you've delivered those two series, we'll have 52 shows.'

'So?'

'52 - it's a magic number. There's a programme for each week of the year. This means it'll be syndicated all round the world, Europe, the States, on cable and satellite for years and years.'

'So?'

'And then once it's syndicated the show will have a profile world-wide and we'll be able to raise the money for a Red Dwarf Movie.'

He knew I wanted to make movies.

I changed tack. 'But the fans hated VI.'

'No, they didn't. Stop reading the SF press.'

'They really, really hated it, Charles. The only people who liked it were me and Rob.'

'You're exaggerating. I liked it too.'

'I am not doing another series of Red Dwarf. It's the hardest show on television to make, the budget's always lousy, I want to do something NEW!!! Besides, without Rob it won't be the same.'

'I'll say "yes" then, shall I?'

'No, don't say "yes" say "no".'

'Just let me do a budget. I'll make it look so expensive the BBC will say "no" and then you're off the hook.'

'Then I'll be off the hook?'

'You'll be off the hook.'

I agreed.


Two months later. Another phone call. It was Charles again.

I've just heard from the BBC, and they've said "yes".

'Yes to what?'

'Yes, to Series VII.'

'But you said they'd say "no".

Laughter. 'I was wrong.'

'But you said you'd put in a ridiculously expensive budget and they'd say "no".

'Well, yes, but obviously I had to put in a budget that was sensibly ridiculous.'

'Sensibly ridiculous?'

Yes, I mean, if I'd put in a budget that was ridiculously ridiculous they'd have thought I was mad. So I put in a sensibly ridiculous one. Which they thought was too much and they want to get it down a bit but in theory they've said "yes".

'I want to do something new.'

'All the cast are really keen, especially Craig.'

'Craig's in prison.' Pause. 'What about Chris?'

'He might not be absolutely 100 per cent available but we'll cross that bridge when we come to it.'

'What do you mean: not absolutely 100 per cent available?' Is this in any way connected with that interview he gave in *Starlog* where he said: 'Wild horses won't drag me back for another series of Red Dwarf.'

'He was tired when he gave that interview.'

'It was ten in the morning.'

A month passes.

Charles posts me various letters from fans pleading for another series. I'm convinced he's writing them himself with his left hand.

More letters.

More months.

Charles: 'You won't have to write them all, we'll get other writers, all you have to do is bring the team together and oversee it all.'

Bringing in other writers. I'm very unsure. Will they be prepared to re-write as much as Rob and I re-wrote? Draft after draft, right up to the moment of shooting. Will they know the characters? Will they care as much as we used to care? I don't know but, before I realize it, I've agreed to make Red Dwarf VII.

'Who do you want to direct it?'

I have a short list of one - Ed Bye.

It was essential to get Ed back.

Ed and I had worked very closely on the early series, editing and dubbing them together. The edit for me played a huge part in shaping the shows. In a way it was like the final re-write.

A memory I'll never forget - editing the shrinking boxer shorts sequence from Polymorph. Ed and I hysterical, the editor muttering: 'This is disgusting, you can't let this go out, it's disgusting.'

The more he disapproved the more we laughed.

Laughter that made my rib-cage ache.

I staggered out of the room, saying I'd go and get some pizzas. I crossed the road laughing, ordered pizzas laughing, collected pizzas laughing and returned still laughing. I don't think I've ever laughed longer or louder or more uncontrollably at anything in my entire life than that night I went to get those pizzas.

Ed is the best director I've ever worked with and one of the funniest people I've ever met.

If Ed says 'no', then all bets are off.

We meet in a pub.

Instantly, it's like old times. He tells me this story of how a friend of his went skiing and fell madly in love with the ski instructor. One day she's out on her own, slaloming away, when she has to take a pee. There's no-one around so she skids to a halt behind a tree, braves the elements, ski pants down, squats and attends to the call of nature.

Suddenly, half way through, she loses balance and finds herself slowly moving down the slope.

She can't get up.

Still in her squat position.

Pants round ankles, gathering speed.

She's helpless.

She caroms down the slope past the ski lodge where the jet set sit knocking back Schnapps. Including her ski instructor. The one she's in love with.

She howls past leaving a stream of pee and an echoey scream.

Ed swears the story is true and tells me her name. It's someone famous.

Five pints later I get to the point. 'There's going to be a Red Dwarf movie with the British cast, and I want you to direct it.'

'I thought you wanted to do something new.'

'Shut up.'

A pause from Ed. 'A Red Dwarf movie that could be great. I've always wanted to direct movies.'

'Only one catch. We've got to make sixteen new episodes before we do the movie.'

He calls the next day to say 'yes'.

One down.

My next task was to try and persuade Chris to return.

The reasons Chris wanted to leave in the first place were fairly straightforward.

Red Dwarf is the toughest series to make on British television.

The hours are incredibly long; we shoot in terrible locations; we use a lot of blue screen so the actors are often acting alone or with things which will later be added in the edit and compared to the average sit-com it's hell on a stick. Plus the small budget means we're always having to cut corners so the script changes endlessly to save money and again most actors hate countless script modifications and last-minute changes of schedule.

One of the ways we used to persuade Chris to come back was to shoot Series VII without an audience. Chris had grown to dread the nerve-shredding fear of performing live.

Ed was particularly keen to shoot it this way too. He believed, rightly I think, that it would be a great dress rehearsal for the movie. We would be bound to learn things that we couldn't possibly know, never having shot the series in this way before. In shows like 'Gunmen of the Apocalypse', half the show had been shot without an audience, fifteen minutes being recorded and then played in to the live studio audience with the other fifteen minutes live, but never more than this.

For Series VII Chris agreed to be available for three weeks and I thought if he enjoyed the new way of making Red Dwarf then maybe he'd be interested in returning full time for Series VIII and the film.

I toyed with the idea of replacing him temporarily with another actor but rejected this, again with an eye on the future, believing if I did recast, then Chris would be less keen than ever to return full time.

A lot of the fans, I know, thought I'd gone bonkers and replaced Rimmer with Kochanski. This was never the intention, Chloë had joined the crew for entirely different reasons. The movie people I'd spoken to had made it pretty clear a 'gorgeous actress' was essential if we were to raise sufficient funds to make the film and retain the British cast. I thought the idea of making a film with an all star American cast was pointless. I wanted to retain the gang and this was the one sweetener I had to throw the way of the movie moguls.

The plan worked. Chris enjoyed the new way of making the series so much he returned to Series VIII full time, even agreeing to the dreaded live recordings.

I was thrilled.

It was great to have him back.

One of my favourite Chris stories happened during the making of Series IV. Chris is an absolute car nut and at one point had about thirty cars. Bentleys, Jags, World War II Land Rovers, you name it. He even had three Range Rovers all different years because he enjoyed comparing the way the gears changed in the gear box.

Honestly.

At one point he was looking for a house with a drive-in sitting room, so he could park all his cars inside his house. I know you don't believe any of this but I swear to you it's true.

One rehearsal day, a guest star sat around rather glumly as we waited for Ed to finalise his camera positions and Craig asked him if he was OK? The Guest Star said he was going through a bit of a rough time at the moment, everyone went quiet not wanting to pry.

Craig, chipper as ever, piped up: 'Why's that?'

The Guest Star said: 'Well, I've decided to leave home. I've met someone else, so this morning I packed my bags and left. I've left my wife of over twenty years, my two lovely daughters, my house, my dog, the lot. Everything I have in the world I walked away from this morning. All I have now are the clothes I stand up in and a suitcase with a few possessions. I felt so guilty about leaving I've even left my BMW in the garage.'

Everyone stared at the floor, contemplating this tragic situation.

Finally, an ashen faced Chris broke the silence: 'You left your BMW?' he asked incredulously.

Everyone roared, including the Guest Star, who seemed to cheer up a bit after that.


Doug Naylor

# INTRODUCTION
## BACK IN THE RED - PART ONE.

'The budget for Red Dwarf VIII was almost identical to the budget of Victoria Wood's *dinnerladies*.
When I was told this I went around telling everyone who'd listen.
I expected them to gasp in disbelief.
Instead something else happened. Everyone I told raised an eyebrow about half a millimetre - even Roger Moore in his hey day would have looked more animated. This wasn't the reaction I wanted at all.
No-one seemed surprised. And then I realised. The truth was very simple. No-one, but no-one, believed me.
They didn't believe me because it wasn't possible for the show to look as good as it did with a sit-com budget.
But it's true.
Is anyone listening?
On Red Dwarf VIII we had an almost identical budget to *dinnerladies*. Someone please be astounded.

For the first seven series of Red Dwarf the special effects for the series were largely controlled by Peter Wragg and his BBC special effects team. Just before Series VII began Peter was promoted to Manager of BBC Visual Effects and was no longer able to take a day to day interest in the running of that side of the series. Instead he was in charge of making the BBC Visual Effects Department cost effective.
For the first time the BBC VFX department had to make a profit or at very least break even with every project they did. It soon became apparent that a BBC programme with a budget funded by the BBC and BBC World-wide, the BBC's videos and overseas arm, could no longer afford to use the BBC VFX department!!
This was largely due to the overheads every BBC department has to carry.
An example: we asked how much it would cost to make a Skutter - I wanted the Skutters to return if at all possible in the new series and we were told a single Skutter would cost somewhere in the region of £35,000 and ideally I wanted three.
I adored working with Peter over the years and it was heart breaking to realize we would have to go somewhere else if we wanted the show to continue to develop in this area. But with the new constraints Peter was working under we had no choice. Ironically, we could no longer have afforded the BBC VFX department if we'd been making the *first* series now, costs had risen so steeply.

Instead we went to Jim Francis, who used to work for the BBC VFX department but was now freelance and he took care of all the explosions, animatronics and miniatures (using a motion controlled camera rig) working alongside Bill Pearson (*Alien*, *Lost in Space* and John Travolta's *BattleField Earth*). The third main member of the team was Chris Veale, a twenty-four-year-old wunderkind who worked from home, (in a room that used to be his bedroom. No snazzy West End post production houses for us.)
Chris Veale was responsible for all the CGI on Series VIII.
Between Jim, Chris and Bill, and at amazingly low cost, they produced the best special effects the show has ever had.
Ever.

The small budget means that constantly we have to make compromises. We simply can't afford to shoot the show we want because we haven't got the money or the time. That's why the three parter 'Back in the Red' may never be seen in the shape it was originally intended, which was a slightly long one hour special. And why 'Pete' became a two parter and why we lost what I intended to be the final show of the series, an episode entitled 'Earth'.

Red Dwarf VIII started life in the sound dub of Series VII. Ed and I were slumped at the back of the sound booth, sprouting five day growths and wondering whether we'd ever see daylight again. The day usually began at around 9.30 and finished, a small ocean of coffee later, at around two or three the following morning.
I hadn't been happy with certain aspects of VII and started making a list of changes for the next series.
The experiment with new writers hadn't worked as well as we'd hoped.
The new series, I decided, I wanted to write mostly myself, but keeping Paul Alexander's input.
Rob still wasn't interested in returning. Chris, however, did agree to return.
I persuaded the production crew to re-introduce the live audience.
And the Dwarfers returned to the Dwarf.
Going into the series I felt at last we had a chance of making one of the best series we'd ever made.
My hands were no longer tied.
We were playing on an even playing field with both Chris and Norman returning full time.

# RED DWARF VIII

## 'BACK IN THE RED - PART 1'

### EPISODE 1

## Written by
## DOUG NAYLOR

18

# BACKINTHERED
## PART ONE.

### TITLES

**1 INT. CGI SEQUENCE DAY**
Prison establisher.

**2 INT. PRISON QUARTERS – DAY**
Lister lies in his bunk reading a showbiz mag. Rimmer in his bunk reading a novel.

**LISTER**
Remember Argyle Sommerfield, the old movie star? 83 according to this, and he's just had a baby with his nurse.

~~83? At that age you're usually,~~ considered sprightly if you go to the toilet in the right room, never mind anything else.

He goes back to his mag.

**LISTER**
Look at her, she's gorgeous. How do you impress someone like that when you're 83? By doing what? Taking her for a ride on your Stannah Stairlift? Sunday afternoon, wind in her hair, bombing up stairs at a quarter of a mile an hour - it can obviously turn a girl's ~~head.~~ 'It was love at first sight,' she cooed. 'I've always liked older men'. God, if she ever ran into Tutankhamun he wouldn't stand a chance. She'd have his bandages off before you could say: silicon implants. There's a picture of them here with the new born. There's Argyle, and there's the baby. No, no, no, no, there's Argyle and there's the baby. I was thrown for a minute by the bib and the bonnet - I thought that was the baby at first.

He goes back to his mag. Rimmer moves to table.

**LISTER**
An 83 year old Dad? How is that going to work? I bet he's not going to get up in the middle of the night to help give the baby its feeds. He'll probably pretend to be dead. 'Darling, can you give the baby his bottle tonight ...'

Lister mimes ghoulish 'dead face'.

**LISTER**
It's not going to work, is it? The only advantage as far as I can see is the wife can change both their nappies at the same time.

**Pause.**

**LISTER**
Are you still not talking to me?

Silence.

**LISTER**
It's unbelievably childish, you know. I've a good mind to fill your shoes with runny porridge again. That'd teach you a lesson about maturity.

Silence.

**LISTER**
All right, I'll tell you what - I bet I can make you say something in the next minute.

**Silence.**

**LISTER**
Twenty big ones.

**Silence.**

**LISTER**
Shake on it.

**Silence.**

**LISTER**
All right, well, if I'm on: say nothing.

**Silence.**

**LISTER**
I'm on. OK, I'm going to say something all right and you're going to totally lose it. Are you ready? Are you ready?

**Silence.**

**LISTER**
All right. Several years ago, when money was not abundant and I needed, I mean, medically needed, a pint, I took some money from your purse.

**Mimes opening creaking purse.**

**LISTER**
Oh God, it was horrible going in there, the wallet

that time forgot. Not that there was any point, barman on B Deck wouldn't serve me - said doubloons weren't legal tender anymore. Said you should've handed them in after the Spanish Armada.

**Silence.**

**LISTER**
I thought that'd get you going. You hate digs about your stinginess. Usually makes you so agitated that you gotta go and make a cup of tea with a brand new tea bag.

**Silence.**

**LISTER**
Well, still plenty of time to go. **(Laughs)** Remember Yvonne McGruder?

**Silence**

**LISTER**
You really liked her, didn't you?

**Silence**

**LISTER**
I used to go out with her, you know? Before you did. You didn't know that did you?

**Silence.**

**LISTER**
We broke up in the end, really hurt me. Still got the scars today - they never heal carpet burns, do they?

**LISTER**
Both cheeks, man - she nearly wore them down to the bone.

*Lister miming gyrations.*

**RIMMER**
Will you shut up!!

**LISTER**
What did I tell you? Twenty big ones.

**RIMMER**
I have been listening to you whittling on now for what seems like two ice ages. My mind is so numb and brain dead I feel like I've just attended a 3-day seminar entitled "The Future of Plumbing".

**RIMMER**
Have you any idea how irritating you've just been? You're a master. There are things you could teach to tropical skin diseases.

**LISTER**
Well, talk to me then.

**RIMMER**
No.

**LISTER**
Look, I'm sorry, OK? How many times do you want me to say it? I am sorry.

**RIMMER**
No, you're not.

**LISTER**
It was an accident.

**RIMMER**
An accident? You poured a whole tube of it over me, you disgusting, rotting, fetid, piece of congealed monkey vomit!

**LISTER**
(**Happy**) At last you're talking to me. I knew we'd

make it up.

*Lister picks up magazine and starts reading.*

**LISTER**
83!!!

## 3  BLACK SCREEN
Caption: 'Three Days earlier'.

## 4  EXT. CGI/MODEL SEQUENCE (RECAP SERIES VII)
**Starbug flies into Red Dwarf, through the landing bay.**

**CAT**
Thing's even bigger than I remember. Er ... guys, we got a problem.

## 5 INT. CGI/MODEL SEQUENCE
**Starbug passes a giant hand rail and a control panel, signs etc. and heads towards an open door way.**

## 6 INT. STARBUG COCKPIT - DAY
**Lister steps in - his body back to normal.**

**LISTER**
Hey, guys, look at my body!

**CAT**
There's an invitation that will not cause a stampede.

**LISTER**
No, it's back to normal.

**KRYTEN**
No time for that now, sir. We're flying down a corridor on Red Dwarf and Starbug appears to be expanding.

**KOCHANSKI**
It's not Starbug that's expanding, it's Red Dwarf that's shrinking.

**LISTER**
It must be something to do with the Nanobot molecular process, just like my body.

## 7 CGI/MODEL SEQUENCE
**Starbug enters the corridor.**
**The walls move slightly as they contract.**

**The ship passes the camera and continues down the corridor.**

**As Starbug passes an airvent, it is too small to escape the air flow and starts to get sucked in.**

## 8 INT.STARBUG COCKPIT - DAY

**CAT**
We're being sucked into a vent, can't fight it.

## 9 CGI/MODEL SEQUENCE
**The bug gets sucked in and narrowly avoids the rotating blades as it enters the vent.**

**Having regained control, the bug flies down the vent, the cam tracking with it. The shrinking air-vent walls closing in on the ship.**

## 10 INT. STARBUG COCKPIT - DAY

**KOCHANSKI**
Air-vent walls closing in.

**KRYTEN**
We must take action, be bold, positive, decisive. Suggest we move from blue alert to red alert, sir.

**CAT**
Forget red, let's go all the way up to brown alert.

**KRYTEN**
There's no such thing as brown alert, sir.

**CAT**
You won't be saying that in a minute. And don't say I didn't alert you.

**Holly appears on screen.**

**HOLLY**
All right, dudes. Anyone fancy a game of charades using just your nose? Or is this a bad time?

**LISTER**

Holly, we're about to get crushed to death.

**HOLLY**

That's a 'no' then, is it?

**KRYTEN**

Once the Nanos rebuilt the ship I thought things were going to get back to normal.

**KOCHANSKI**

We don't know where we are, what to do and haven't a clue what's happening. Things are back to normal.

**HOLLY**

You don't even fancy a bit of a quick one? Science fiction film, name of the ship, one word.

**He raises his nose in the air and makes spooky noises.**

**HOLLY**

The Nostrilomo. Spent a week thinking that one up. Good, innit?

**KRYTEN**

Computing time to impact ... calculations coming through ... here they come.

**LISTER**

How long have we got?

**KRYTEN**

About the time it takes to read a 'Stop' sign, sir.

**CAT**

That's OK then, I don't always get through those in one sitting.

**KOCHANSKI**

What are our chances of us getting out of here?

**KRYTEN**

About the same odds as discovering Mr Lister saddle stitching the hem of a pair of lemon maternity slacks.

**LISTER**

I must admit, it's been a while since I did that. Can't you get this crate to go faster. It's going to be like getting crushed to death in a gigantic trouser press.

**CAT**

Freshly laundered and wrinkle free. I always prayed I'd go out like that.

**KOCHANSKI**

There's maybe a way through this, if we take a detour, past Epsilon 14 and take a right at the hydro unit, we'll save about two minutes.

**KRYTEN**

What do you say, sir? I don't understand a woman who's hurtling towards thirty and still has a teddy bear called Boo-boo but when it comes to navigation there's none finer.

**LISTER**

What's your view, Hol?

**HOLLY**

Straight up your nose when you lean in like that.

**LISTER**

Epsilon 14.

## 11 CGI/MODEL SEQUENCE

**Starbug does a U-turn in the air-vent and crashes through another fan. It bounces off the air-vent walls, losing engine housings.**

**We see an air-vent grate. We hear an approaching rumbling sound. Suddenly Starbug explodes through the grating and surrounding wall and flies off down the corridor, as rubble and dust disperse behind.**

**We follow the damaged Starbug down the shrinking corridor. As space gets tighter, the bug veers to the side and hits the wall. And rebounds impacting the other wall.**

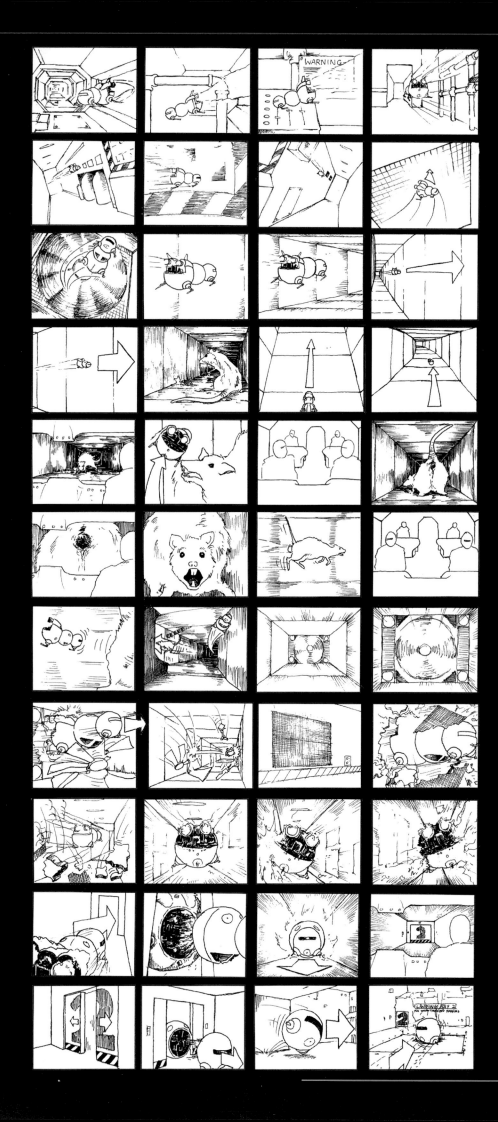

## 12 INT. STARBUG - DAY

Posse as before.

**KRYTEN**
There's some kind of heart beat up ahead and it's beating at an incredible rate.

**CAT**
You mean there's a heart out there with no body? No wonder it's beating so fast.

They dodge one rat and fly into the bum of another.

**HOLLY**
Hope we don't get stopped by the cops - they don't like it when you're rat arsed.

They fly for some time with rat on the front before reversing off it and sending it sailing off down a corridor.

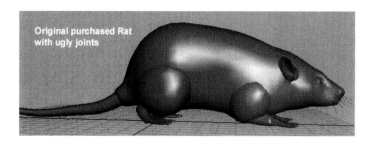
Original purchased Rat with ugly joints

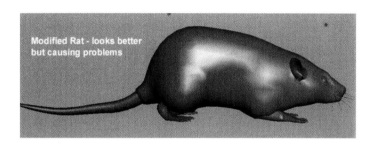
Modified Rat - looks better but causing problems

Starbug flies through a door and the shrinking walls rip off the rear bubble of the ship.

## 13 INT. STARBUG COCKPIT - DAY

**CAT**
According to the desk we've lost all the engines, didn't I read somewhere that can seriously affect your ability to fly?

## 14 CGI/MODEL SEQUENCE

Starbug flies through the Landing Bay door and the shrinking walls rip off the mid-section of the ship.

## 15 INT. STARBUG COCKPIT - DAY

**KRYTEN**
Now we've lost the mid-section and the kitchen. I'm sorry everyone but we may have to have sandwiches for lunch.

## 16 CGI/MODEL SEQUENCE

The last remaining bubble of Starbug crashes into the Landing Bay, skids along the floor and comes to a halt.

## 17 INT. STARBUG COCKPIT - DAY

Flames and smoke. Kochanski lies on the floor unconscious.

**LISTER**
There's a pulse. But maybe I should give her the kiss of life to be on the safe side.

**KRYTEN**
Isn't the kiss of life for drowning, sir?

**LISTER**
Nitpicker.

Kochanski comes round and smiles sweetly at him.

**KOCHANSKI**
Is everyone OK?

**LISTER**
No, I'm not. I'm really frustrated.

**KRYTEN**
Sir, come quickly, the Cat looks terrible.

**CAT**
Terrible? Your eyes need a major service, bud.

**KRYTEN**
I mean you look good, sir. Great in fact, handsome, stylish and cooler than a cucumber in a designer suit sipping dry Martini on a schooner. But you're badly hurt.

**CAT**
For a second, I thought it was serious.

**LISTER**
Let's get him out of here before the whole thing goes up.

## 18 EXT. STARBUG COCKPIT BUBBLE - DAY

The airlock door swings open and they stagger out and run towards the camera as the cockpit blows up behind throwing them to the ground.

Several men in masks loom over them. They pull off their masks. Chen and Selby from Series 1, EP 1 among others.

**SELBY**
Dave?

**LISTER**
Selby? Chen?
Is it really you?

**CHEN**
(To Selby)
Is it really us?
Hang on, I'll check.

He feels himself quickly all over.

**CHEN**
Yeah, I think it's us.

Lister hugs them.

**LISTER**
Guys, this is brilliant. I can't believe it.

**KRYTEN**
You know these people, Sir?

**LISTER**
Know them - when they've been drunk and unconscious, I've taken their clothes off and painted parts of them green. Of course I know them. This is the Red Dwarf crew, Krytie.

**CAT**
How?

**KOCHANSKI**
The Nanos must have resurrected them along with the ship.

**LISTER**
This is Chen, he works in the kitchen and he's always drunk and this is Selby and he's always drunk too. Where's Petersen?

**CHEN**
He couldn't make it. He's drunk.

**KRYTEN**
The crew are all alive, sir. This is great news. Wonderful, marvellous incredible news. All that extra ironing - bliss.

Hollister breaks through the group.

**HOLLISTER**
Mr Thornton, read them their rights.

**MP THORNTON**
David Lister, you are formally charged with stealing and crashing a Starbug, you are also charged with having no pilot's licence and smuggling two stowaways on board along with Navigation Officer Kristine Kochanski. Anything you say now or do not say now may be used in a board of enquiry against you. Do you require any form of aid?

**LISTER**
Yeah, lemonade in a really large scotch.

**CHEN**
Don't worry, Davey. Me, Petersen, and Selbs, we'll stick by you, son. You may have nicked a Starbug and tried to drive it down a corridor and then crash landed it into a 2 billion dollar computer network but there was nothing malacious in it. It's just because you're a moron. The jury'll understand that.

**SELBY**
You learn who you mates are in situations like this. We'll stand by you, man.

**CHEN**
Your old drinking buddies. We'll be there for you, fighting your corner, through thick and thin, rain or shine, obviously so long as it doesn't clash with our drinking commitments. **(To Selby)** Come on, we're going to get him the best damned lawyer money can buy.

**SELBY**
**(Looks at watch)** Bar's just opened.

**CHEN**
What a terrible piece of luck for poor old Davey.

*They go off to the bar.*

## 19 INT. CORRIDOR OUTSIDE SLEEPING QUARTERS - DAY
Two MPs escort Lister to his quarters.

**MP THORNTON**
Left, right, left, right, left, right, left, right.

**LISTER**
You want to try and relax. You're going to burst a blood vessel.

**MP THORNTON**
Shut up, you maggot!! Do you understand? DO YOU UNDERSTAND?

**LISTER**
Yes.

**MP THORNTON**
Yes, what!!?

**LISTER**
Yes, Mr Shouty?

**MP THORNTON**
Yes, sir!!!!

## 20 INT. LISTER'S SLEEPING QUARTERS - DAY
Thornton escorts him in.

**MP THORNTON**
(Out of shot) Left, right, left, right, left, right
(Enters quarters) left, right, left, right, left, right,
HALT!! ... Left arm.

Thornton fits security bracelet.

**MP THORNTON**
At ease.

Thornton leaves.
Lister adjusts his watch - and Holly materializes.

**HOLLY**
All right, dude?

**LISTER**
They don't know about you yet, Hol, it might be an idea to keep it that way. I need some info.
If the board of enquiry finds us guilty tomorrow - what happens then?

**HOLLY**
Well, they'll probably have a pot of tea, bit of a chat and go home I suppose.

**LISTER**
What happens to us, you divvy? Not them.

**HOLLY**
Well, if you lose you'll probably get a couple of years in the brig.

**LISTER**
What brig?

**HOLLY**
The brig on Floor 13.

**LISTER**
There isn't a Floor 13.

**HOLLY**
Yeah, there is. It was classified. A need to know only basis.

**LISTER**
So who knew?

**HOLLY**
Well, all the officers and anyone who's ever seen *The Twilight Zone*.

**LISTER**
So, what's it like this brig?

**HOLLY**
Well, if I was an estate agent I'd probably describe it as an old style penal establishment, abundant wild-life, two hundred bedrooms, all with ensuite buckets.

**LISTER**
Smegging hell.

**HOLLY**
They call it the Tank. There was a inmate population of 400, all being transported to Adelphi 12. Presumably they've all been resurrected too.

**LISTER**
What are they like? No, don't tell me. I already know. They're all deranged, hairy, no lobbers, breath like old nappies, arms like toilet walls, scum of the universe. They're all like that, aren't they?

**HOLLY**
Well, the nice ones are, yeah. Hang on, I've got one of them on file somewhere. Here we go.

**Man appears on screen**

**NIGEL**
I'm Nigel, I'm nice.

**HOLLY**
See what I mean, they're not all headbangers. Nige is lovely, though he does tend to get a bit narky if you go too close to him with a magnet.

**LISTER**
Thanks very much, Hol, you're really cheering me up.

**Lister turns Holly off.**

**LISTER**
The brig, two years. Two years without curry and lager. Two years without sex ...

**RIMMER**
You hope.

**Lister turns and sees Rimmer.**

**LISTER**
Rimmer?

**RIMMER**
Word's out, they're going to throw the book at you, Listy, followed by the bookcase and then the library, brick by brick.

**LISTER**
God, it's you like you used to be. Ugh.

**RIMMER**
What got into you? You can't fly a Starbug, milado, you're a technician, a zero, a nobody.

**LISTER**
Look, this is going to sound nuts but the whole crew died, including you. And you've all been resurrected by these microscopic little robots.

**RIMMER**
I died?

**LISTER**
Yeah.

**RIMMER**
All the crew died?

**LISTER**
Yeah.

**RIMMER**
And you are going to spend the next two years in the brig with a load of neanderthals with badly spelt tattoos? So where are we? Is this my heaven?

**LISTER**

Look, a radiation leak wiped everybody out.
I survived cos I was in Stasis, then these Nanos
arrived, rebuilt the ship and resurrected the crew.

**RIMMER**

So where are they?

**LISTER**

Don't know. Gone. Scarpered. Maybe we should
take the fifth?

**RIMMER**

The fifth? If I were you, I'd take the sixth,
seventh and eight, too.

**LISTER**

I've got to track down these Nanos to corroborate our story. Otherwise who's going to believe
our defence? Only meths drinkers and The Corn
Circle Society. I need your help, man.

**RIMMER**

Me?

Lister indicates controller harness.

**LISTER**

Who else is going to help me? I'm confined to
quarters. The minute I walk through that door I
get enough wattage up my jacksy to light up the
whole of Bootle.

**RIMMER**

Well, considering what the future has in store for
your jacksy, a couple of zillion volts is going to be
easy street.

## 21 INT. CORRIDOR - DAY

Kochanski and Kryten are escorted down a
corridor by two guards. Kryten writing on pad.

**KOCHANSKI**

Why have the Nanobots done this? Put us in this
situation?

**KRYTEN**

In the past they've only ever done things which
have ultimately benefited us. We should take
comfort in that.

**KOCHANSKI**

Like what?

**KRYTEN**

Like when they first stole Red Dwarf and took
us on a merry goose chase half way round the
galaxy. They lead us to Legion where Mr Rimmer
acquired a hard light body.

**KOCHANSKI**

Benefit.

**KRYTEN**

And then they took us back to Red Dwarf and
rebooted Holly.

**KOCHANSKI**

Benefit. And after that they led you to the
temporal rip where you met me.

Kryten throws away his pad.

## 22 INT. CORRIDOR - DAY

Doc Newton stands outside the men's toilet waiting.
The door opens and Captain Hollister backs out
spraying the loo with air freshener.

**DOC NEWTON**

What's this rumour that we're 3 million light
years into deep space and Red Dwarf's changed
shape?

**HOLLISTER**

That is classified information, Karen. Who the
hell told you that?

**DOC NEWTON**

The coffee machine on G Deck.

**HOLLISTER**

Damned coffee machine. I'm going to bust his
ass down to a tampon dispenser.

**DOC NEWTON**
Is it true?

**HOLLISTER**
Until we get Holly back up, we can't verify it. Starbug took out one of its CPU banks in the crash and we're having trouble rebooting.

**DOC NEWTON**
The coffee machine said the ship's now identical to its original design plans. Before the JMC made all its cut backs?

**HOLLISTER**
We now have a quark-level matter/antimatter generator, ship-wide bio-organic computer networking and a karaoke bar on C Deck.

**DOC NEWTON**
But how, and how did we wind up in deep space?

**HOLLISTER**
Nobody knows. ~~It's going to go down in history~~ as one of the great mysteries to rank alonside the ~~Marie Celeste and the popularity of broccoli.~~

**23 INT. MEDI-BAY - DAY**
On a monitor we see:- Medi-Scan enabled. Abnormalities detected. Cardiovascular system and internal ...

Hollister and Doc Newton arrive at the Cat recovering in bed.

**DOC NEWTON**
We don't believe this one's human. Take a look at this -

**Pulls back sheet. We don't see.**

**HOLLISTER**
Has he got the measles?

**DOC NEWTON**
No, those are his nipples, Frank.

**HOLLISTER**
Six nipples? I wonder what the female of the species is like?

**CAT**
Pretty easy to please in bed, especially if you play the piano.

**DOC NEWTON**
His internal organs are different too.

**Look at monitor.**

**HOLLISTER**
In what way?

**DOC NEWTON**
Well, his kidney, liver, appendix are all colour co-ordinated. And even weirder, his stomach wall appears to be decorated.

**HOLLISTER**
This guy's intestines look better than my quarters.

**DOC NEWTON**
His heart beat's weird too. Instead of a normal heart beat, his sounds - cooler.

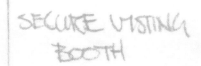

**CAT**

You think I'm gonna have the dorky human heart beat? Bum, bum, bum, bum - where's the tune in that?

**HOLLISTER**

Let me hear it.

**Doc turns up sound. They listen to the Cat's cool heart beat.**

**DOC NEWTON**

Also his pulse has a different rhythm.

**Cat's heart and pulse play some Blues riff. Hollister starts to jig to the music.**

**HOLLISTER**

Hell, that's good, can you slam that down on tape for me?

## 24 INT. CORRIDOR - DAY

**Lister and Rimmer sit outside the medical centre. Two guards sit some distance away.**

**LISTER**

Rimmer, I'm begging you, man, help me escape. I've got to track down these Nanobots.

**RIMMER**

I'm not risking my career and standing for you, Listy. I'm going places ...

**LISTER**

(L impersonates R) ... up the ziggurat. Lickety split.

**RIMMER**

... up the ziggurat. Lickety split. Precisely. I'm going to pass the engineering exam ...

**LISTER**

(L impersonates R) ... and become an officer.

**RIMMER**

... and become an officer. Yes. An officer, a guy of honour, decency and breeding.

**LISTER**

You saying - I haven't got those qualities?

**RIMMER**

Generally, people with breeding - when they're bored and want my bridge club chums to wrap up and go home, people with breeding, generally do not play 'Popeye the Sailor Man' with a kazoo inserted between their buttocks.

**LISTER**

I remember that. (Laughs) I used to do that sort of thing, didn't I?

**RIMMER**

And while we're on the subject, when someone's had a tad too much claret and has fallen asleep, naked on their bunk, people of honour generally don't take a polaroid of your snoozing todger, draw a moustache, mouth and ears on it, and then pin it up on the bulletin board under missing persons!! They don't write underneath: have you seen this man? Believed to be a French movie star!

**LISTER**

As if your todger with a couple of eyes drawn on it would look like a French movie star. Way too good looking.

**RIMMER**

Don't expect help from me, Lister.

**LISTER**

But that was years ago.

**RIMMER**

It was last week.

**LISTER**

Yeah, last week for you because you've just been resurrected, years ago for me. And anyway, I was wurlitzed then. I'd even finished off the Advocaat. I'd even downed that smeg awful pink stuff at the back of the drinks cabinet.

**RIMMER**

That was my Windolene. I must have left it there when I was cleaning the glass.

**LISTER**

It tasted all right with that chartreuse green liqueury thing in it.

**RIMMER**

You drank my Swarfega too? You're unbelievable.

**LISTER**

Look I've changed. I'm different now. More mature, more debonair - I don't even stir my tea with a spanner anymore, you'd hardly recognize me.

**RIMMER**

Have you stopped playing the guitar?

**LISTER**

No, but I've stopped accompanying myself on my armpit. What I'm trying to say is I don't have to take my frustrations out on you anymore.

**RIMMER**

How's that?

**LISTER**

Well, I've been away, what is it? Five, six years, not counting Stasis, I've done stuff. Stuff that would make your hair straight. I've come through it. **(Beat)** I can help you.

**RIMMER**

Do what?

**LISTER**

Get promoted.

**RIMMER**

Preposterous. How?

**LISTER**

Information. I've seen the crew's confidential reports. I've seen their strengths and weaknesses.

**RIMMER**

How?

**LISTER**

Well, before you were resurrected I had the run of the whole of the ship. I've seen the crew's files, medical records, sessions with the therapist, the works. 'Knowledge is power.' Who said that?

**RIMMER**

I don't know.

**LISTER**

Nor do I. **(Pause)** The point I'm trying to make is: I can make you look like a genius. You'll get promoted in the field, man. You won't have to take exams, do that astro-engineering smeg. Just help me escape.

**Rimmer thinks about it.**

**RIMMER**

I have my principles, Lister, you think you can buy me with promises of power and glory? You really think ... OK, I'll do it. But you'll have to prove it to me first.

**LISTER**

You're on.

**RIMMER**

Get me promoted.

**LISTER**

You've got it.

**RIMMER**

OK, deal.

**Lister takes off his Holly watch.**

**LISTER**

You'll find the confidential files in Starbug's cockpit. There's a senile version of Holly loaded into this watch - he'll lead you to it.

**Rimmer takes the watch.**

## 25 INT. THERAPIST'S OFFICE – DAY

**Kryten sits in a chair, screwed into the floor. Establish at top of scene.**

**THERAPIST**
Hello, I'm Dr Lucas McClaren. I'm the ship's Chief Psychiatric Counsellor and I thought it was about time we got together and had a really good natter.

**KRYTEN**
My name is Kryten, sir.

**THERAPIST**
Lovely. We are doing well, aren't we? Now, you're a robot, aren't you?

**KRYTEN**
I was the last time I looked, sir, yes.

**THERAPIST**
And can you tell me when you were created? Can you remember?

**KRYTEN**
2340, sir.

**THERAPIST**
Very good. 2340. Now that's in the future, isn't it?

**KRYTEN**
Yes, sir, I was created after you died.

**THERAPIST**
Lovely. Lovely. So I died and you were created and how long would you say I've been dead altogether?

**KRYTEN**
You're not dead anymore, sir.

**THERAPIST**
Aren't I?

**KRYTEN**
No, no - you're alive again now, sir. Can't you tell?

**THERAPIST**
Right, I was alive, died, and then started living again.

**KRYTEN**
You've been most fortunate, sir.

**THERAPIST**
Golly. **(Charming)** Your chair is screwed down, isn't it, Kryten?

**KRYTEN**
Yes, sir.

**THERAPIST**
Just checking. Excellent. Lovely. Lovely. So, how did I suddenly spring back to life again?

**KRYTEN**
You were rebuilt, sir. By these itty-bitty, teeny-weeny, teenty, little robots.

**THERAPIST**
Teenty little robots?

**KRYTEN**
And they make this little noise.

**Makes Nano noise**

**THERAPIST**
Yes, just double check that chair for me, would you, Kryten? It is still screwed down, isn't it?

**KRYTEN**

Yes, sir.

**THERAPIST**

With really long long screws that go deep deep into the ground?

**KRYTEN**

Yes, sir.

**THERAPIST**

Lovely. Lovely. Now tell me what kind of robot do you think you are? What were you programmed to do?

**KRYTEN**

I'm a Sanitation Droid, sir. I'm programmed to do sanitation type things. Washing, cleaning, ironing.

**THERAPIST**

You also drive space ships though, don't you? Pretend to be the Science Officer, and sit in that lovely swivelly chair with all those lovely pretty buttons and press them all.

**KRYTEN**

Yes, I do that too, sir. That's sort of thanks to Mr Lister.

**THERAPIST**

Mr Lister?

**KRYTEN**

Um yes - he helped me break my programming, sir. Over the years I've managed to develop some serious character faults of which I'm extremely proud. I'm even able to lie to a modest standard. For example, you have a very fine haircut. (**Laughs**) You see how good I've got? Also, I've completely mastered pomposity - even though I say so myself. I've also developed several rudimentary emotions, including fear -

**Kryten suddenly looks scared.**

**KRYTEN**

Oh, my God, it's going to kill us.

**KRYTEN**

Sadness -

**Kryten looks sad.**

**KRYTEN**

Oh, my God, it's killed us. Happiness -

**Kryten looks happy.**

**KRYTEN**

Oh, no it hasn't. Surprise -

**Kryten looks suprised.**

**KRYTEN**

Oh, I've turned into a frog. And just lately I'm proud to say I've got the hang of anger with rudimentary mindless violence -

**Kryten hammers the therapist's little finger with his fist.**

**KRYTEN**

That's a newie. I was going to launch it at this year's Emotions Show. At the moment I'm working on ambivalence, which means feeling two opposite irreconcilable emotions about the same thing.

**Kryten pulls a series of strange expressions.**

**KRYTEN**

As you can see I haven't quite got the hang of that one yet. I look like a dog with a caramel toffee.

**THERAPIST**

What is your relationship with Lister?

**KRYTEN**

I love Mr Lister, sir. He taught me everything. Without him, I'd probably be normal.

**THERAPIST**

I'm going to make a recommendation now, Kryten, which I think will help you. But just before I do, just double check that chair for me would you?

On Kryten's file in the box marked 'Recommended Action', the therapist stamps: 'Restore to factory settings'.

## 26 EXT/INT CARGO BAY - DAY
Rimmer walks across the cargo bay.

## 27 INT. STARBUG COCKPIT - DAY
Rimmer finds CD - Crew Confidential

**RIMMER**
Yes!

Rimmer rifles through some stuff and then two tubes: marked 'Luck Virus' and 'Sexual Magnetism'.

**RIMMER**
'Luck Virus', 'Sexual Magnetism'. Holly, what's this?

**HOLLY**
Dave got them years ago from this Scientist called Lanstrom. They're positive viruses. One gives you sexual magnetism and the other gives you luck. Well, till your natural body defences combat the virus.

Rimmer looks at the two tubes.

**RIMMER**
'Sexual Magnetism'?

**HOLLY**
You going to use it?

**RIMMER**
Is Paris a kind of plaster? You bet I am. A tiny swigette, to see if it works.

Rimmer swigs from the Sexual Magnetism tube.

**RIMMER**
Well, bottoms up. Then bottoms down and hopefully bottoms up again.

He exits.

Holly on screen with text flashing underneath:- 'sickbags on standby!'

## 28 INT. CORRIDOR - DAY
Rimmer walks down the corridor, a group of attractive women stand around chatting, they all beam at him and say 'Hi'.

**RIMMER**
Ladies.

More women. All twinkly, ad lib 'Hi, Arnold.'

**RIMMER**
The world loves a bastard.

## CAPTION: 'TO BE CONTINUED'.

## TITLES.

# BACKINTHERED
## PART ONE.

## *Cast & Crew*

Written by: **DOUG** NAYLOR

Rimmer: **CHRIS** BARRIE  Lister: **CRAIG** CHARLES  Cat: **DANNY** JOHN-JULES

Kryten: **ROBERT** LLEWELLYN  Kochanski: **CHLOË** ANNETT  Holly: **NORMAN** LOVETT

Hollister: **MAC** McDONALD  Chen: **PAUL** BRADLEY  Selby: **DAVID** GILLESPIE

MP Thornton: **KARL** GLENN STIMPSON  Doc Newton: **KIKA** MIRYLEES

Dr McClaren: **ANDY** TAYLOR


Casting Director: **LINDA** GLOVER  Music: **HOWARD** GOODALL

Production Accountant: **MIKE** AMOS  Graphic Designer: **ANDY** SPENCE

General Manager GNP LTD: **HELEN** NORMAN  Location Manager: **KEN** HAWKINS

Production Co-ordinator: **RACHEL** STEWART

Post-Production Co-ordinator: **SIMON** BURCHELL

Stage Manager: **JACQUELINE** ZOPPI-TIGHE  Gaffer: **JOHN** BARKER

Props Master: **PAUL** DE CSERNATONY  Props Buyer: **TIM** YOUNGMAN

Art Director: **IAN** READE-HILL  Vision Mixer: **JOHN** BARCLAY

Engineering Manager: **ALAN** GODLEMAN  Camera Operator: **ANDY** MARTIN

Location Sound: **NIGEL** DAVIS  Sound Supervisor: **JEM** WHIPPEY

Editor: **MARK** WYBOURN  Script Associate: **PAUL** ALEXANDER

Script Supervisor: **GILLIAN** WOOD  First Assistant Director: **JULIE** SYKES

Visual Effects Designer: **JIM** FRANCIS  **Bill** Pearson  **Ed** Smith

Digital Effects Designer: **CHRIS** VEALE  Make Up Designer: **ANDREA** FINCH

Costume Designer: **HOWARD** BURDEN  Line Producer: **JO** BENNETT

Production Designer: **MEL** BIBBY  Director of Photography: **PETER** MORGAN

Executive Producer: **DOUG** NAYLOR  Produced and Directed by: **ED** BYE

# INTRODUCTION
## BACK IN THE RED – PART TWO.

You meet some interesting people on Red Dwarf. I wandered onto the sound stage early one Tuesday afternoon. The camera guys were lugging their cables from one set to another for the scene we were about to shoot and a few extras were sitting in the audience roster. About ten rows back a man with a whirl of green hair and a hundred-and-fifty-two face piercings grinned down at me. If Thomas Harris had just come up with Hannibal Lecter's madder brother this is what he would have looked like. This was the face of undiluted evil.

Craig wandered up. 'Have you seen that bloke with all the shit in his face?' he said incredibly loudly.

I nodded pleasantly at Hannibal's bro and pretended to look for someone bizarre looking. 'No, everyone looks absolutely normal to me.'

'There, man, the crazy looking dude, with the green hair and the silver face. The one it'd take three and half days to get through the airport X-ray machine.'

'For Chrissakes, Craig, keep it down, I've seen him.'

'He's got 152 pieces of shit in his face and apparently he does it because he likes being stared at.'

'Why doesn't he just wear orange trousers?' I wondered.

'You want to meet him?'

I shake my head furiously. 'Bit busy at the moment.'

'He's really nice.'

I fluster. 'No, really, man, I'm meeting Ed in a minute and we've got to do something really important. A blue screen techno thing.'

Craig's not to be put off. He bounds up the stairs and brings John Lynch down to chat.

I promise myself, if he's carrying a bottle of Chianti, I'm out of here.

'Show Doug all your piercings. He's got them everywhere, man.'

John starts to unbuckle his tunic before I stop him.

It turns out John Lynch is 63, has 152 piercings, and used to work in Barclays bank! 9-5, every day for forty-odd years, until he retired.

Then he decided he needed a hobby.

So he got into piercings.

Tomorrow, he tells us, he's going to get some more. He explains he's going for the world record number of metal bits of shit in the face and wants to get into *The Guinness Book of Records*.

'Wouldn't it be easier to eat forty-eight hot dogs in twenty minutes?' I ask.

He says he doesn't like hot dogs. And you meet so many interesting people in the Piercing World. We don't look convinced. 'They're really really nice,' he insists.

'Cliff Richard is nice,' I tell him. 'Wouldn't it be easier to just join the Cliff Richard fan club. I'm sure his fans are incredibly nice plus you can learn to do that "Power to all our Friends" dance, and also the advantage of joining the Cliff fan club is your head doesn't weigh more than Glasgow.' That's gotta be a drag carrying a head around like that. Plus when you die, who wants an urn that sounds like a pair of maracas.

I later send his photograph to my sister, who was single at the time, and say I think I can fix her up.

She doesn't phone back.

She's really finicky my sister.

# RED DWARF VIII

## 'BACK IN THE RED - PART 2'

### EPISODE 2

## Written by
## DOUG NAYLOR

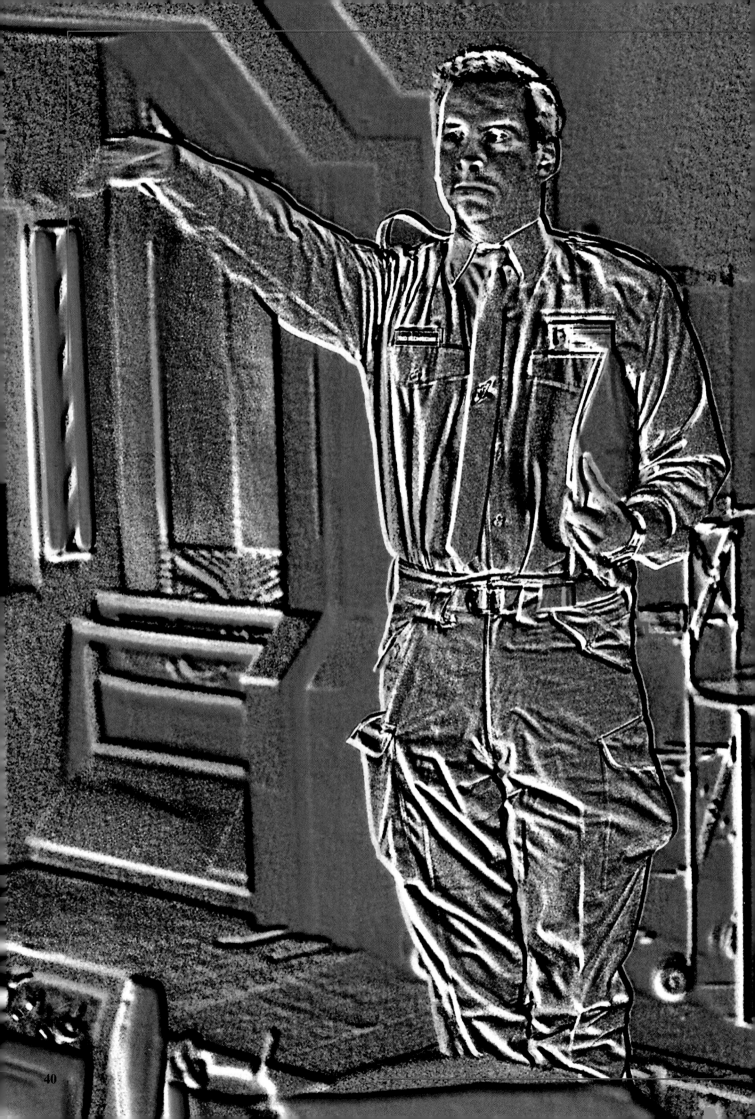

# BACKINTHERED
## PART TWO.

### TITLES

### 1 CGI/MODEL SEQUENCE
**Red Dwarf in space.**

**Text recap:- The mining ship Red Dwarf reconstructed together with its original crew by an army of microscopic robots. Reason - smeg knows!**

### 2 INT. CAPTAIN'S QUARTERS - DAY
**Hollister talks to video diary**

**HOLLISTER**
This is the daily report of the Captain F. Hollister of the mining ship Red Dwarf. Several of my crew are presently being tried for crimes against the Space Corps.

### 3 INT. LISTER'S SLEEPING QUARTERS - DAY (RECAP)
**Lister sitting at table, Rimmer standing by bunks.**

**LISTER**
Look, this is going to sound nuts, but the whole crew died, including you. And you've all been resurrected by these microscopic little robots.

**Time cut to:-**

**LISTER**
I've got to track down these nanos to corroborate our story. Otherwise who's going to believe our defence? Only meths drinkers and The Corn Circle Society. I need your help, man.

**Z** *Script cut from original broadcast.*

### 4 INT. CORRIDOR - DAY (RECAP)
**Lister and Rimmer sit outside the medical centre. Two guards sit some distance away.**

**LISTER**
... I've seen the crew's files, medical records, sessions with the therapist, the works ... I can make you look like a genius. You can get promoted in the field, man. You won't have to take exams ... just help me escape.

**Rimmer thinks about it.**

**RIMMER**
I have my principles, Lister, you think you can buy me with promises of power and glory? You really think ... OK, I'll do it. But you'll have to prove it to me first.

**LISTER**
You're on!

**RIMMER**
Get me promoted.

**Lister takes off Holly watch and passes it to Rimmer.**

**LISTER**
You'll find the confidential files in Starbug's cockpit. There's a senile version of Holly loaded into this watch - he'll lead you to it.

## 5 INT. STARBUG'S COCKPIT DAY (RECAP)

**Rimmer looks around Starbug's burnt out cockpit. He types in a code on the keyboard and a CD is ejected. He takes hold of it.**

**RIMMER**
Yes!

## 6 CGI/MODEL SEQUENCE

**Red Dwarf in space.**

## 7 INT. CAPTAIN'S QUARTERS - DAY

**Hollister is working on some papers, Rimmer marches in and starts one of his extra long salutes.**

**RIMMER**
My Captain, sir.

**HOLLISTER**
Rimmer, is this salute ever going to end - er ... do I have time to go for a cup of coffee? Maybe go on vacation?

**RIMMER**
(Still saluting)
Nearly finished, sir. It's my very special extra long salute I reserve for the especially important, sir.

**HOLLISTER**
You wanted to see me?

**RIMMER**
I'm concerned over some of the safety procedures on board, sir. There's a potentially lethal scenario concerning drive plates, sir. Obviously, anyone who misrepaired one of these plates would have to have a brain the size of a leprechaun's testicle; nevertheless, sir - like German tourists, the stupid are everywhere.
I propose the following new safety procedures sir.

**Rimmer hands Hollister file. Hollister flicks through it.**

**HOLLISTER**
Did you really think of this?

**RIMMER**
Permission to look smug, sir?

**HOLLISTER**
Permission granted.

**Rimmer beams proudly.**

**HOLLISTER**
Good work, Rimmer. Great work.

**RIMMER**
Oh, before I go, sir. Happy Wedding Anniversary, sir.

**Rimmer puts a blueberry muffin on the desk.**

**RIMMER**
I'm sure you must be missing her terribly.

**HOLLISTER**
A blueberry muffin? Like Martha used to make. Thanks, Rimmer. I ... (**Choked up**) Dismiss.

**RIMMER**
Sir, just one more thing. I know the medical guys think we've run out of this stuff but I discovered a couple of unopened medi-crates in Storage, sir. If this is useful to you in any way, it's yours, no questions asked.

**He hands Hollister a tube.**

**HOLLISTER**
Anus-soothe, pile cream. (**Reads**) The easy to apply cream that comes with its own special glove.

Rimmer hands over a glove which fits a single finger.

**RIMMER**
One size fits all. I could tell from your walk.

Hollister takes an envelope and slips a card into it.

**HOLLISTER**
Rimmer, could you post this for me?

Hollister scribbles on envelope.

**RIMMER**
Why, certainly, sir.

Rimmer looks at it.

**RIMMER**
It's addressed to me, sir.

**HOLLISTER**
I'm giving a supper for some of the guys that I've marked out for greater things.

**RIMMER**
And you want me to be the wine waiter, sir?

**HOLLISTER**
This report is first rate. I want you to come to supper. See you on Friday. Incidentally, it's black tie.

**RIMMER**
Thai, Chinese - I'll eat anything, sir. Though I would prefer it if it wasn't black. Any chance of having mine medium rare, sir?

**HOLLISTER**
Just go. Wear what the hell you want.

Rimmer salutes.

## 8 INT. MEDI-BAY - DAY

Kryten enters. Doctor is sitting behind his desk and doesn't look up.

**DOCTOR**
Get undressed. (Points to screen, still not looking up)

Kryten goes behind a screen, we see his lilac suit being draped over the top of the screen. A few clangs. he emerges 'nude'. He is embarrassed and tries to cover himself. Doctor, filling in forms behind a desk doesn't look up as he hands Kryten a urine bottle.

**DOCTOR**
Fill this up, behind the screen.

Kryten goes behind the screen and emerges with the urine bottle full of flowers. Doctor reacts.

Time cut: Doctor wraps blood pressure tube round Kryten's arm and starts to pump. Kryten watches as his left hand starts to inflate. Soon it is three feet long before it finally shoots off and whizzes round the room.

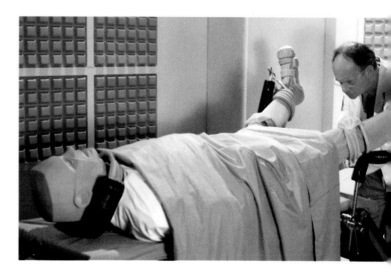

Kryten lies on a couch, his legs in stirrups. The doctor reaches out of shot - he comes back into shot holding a power drill.

Kryten reacts. We hear bolts being unscrewed then dropping onto the floor. Then Kryten's head falls off and rolls out of the door.

## 9 INT. KOCHANSKI'S SLEEPING QUARTERS - DAY

**Guard unlocks the door and Kryten enters.**

**KOCHANSKI**
Kryten, hi. What are you doing here? (**Off his look**) What's wrong?

**KRYTEN**
I've been classified as a woman.

**KOCHANSKI**
A woman? Why?

**KRYTEN**
Well because I haven't got a (**Mouths silently**) penis. It's a Space Corps Directive to prevent gender ambiguity in jail. What's the saying: 'If you've got nothing to swing, you can't be with Bing'?

**KOCHANSKI**
Well, what happened? Did you lose it?

**KRYTEN**
I was never issued with one, ma'am. Why would I need one unless somehow I lost both arms and there was an emergency situation to write my name in the snow. I can't believe it. I used to be Kryten but now I'm Krysten. I sound like the title of an Ed Wood movie.

**KOCHANSKI**
So, you mean, you've never had a steak pie, peas and chips then?

**KRYTEN**
I think the phrase is meat and two veg, ma'am.

**KOCHANSKI**
I knew it was some meal with loads of calories.

**KRYTEN**
The only mechanoids that were ever issued with genitals were the ones created to work on Italian star ships. It was felt they could acclimatize themselves better if they could mimic their Italian crew mates and stand around cupping themselves all day.

**KOCHANSKI**
Hey, now you're a woman it's going to mean some big changes in the way you behave.

**KRYTEN**
I'm not going to be a woman for long, ma'am. Just over-night. They want my permission to repair my corrupted files tomorrow afternoon, restore my factory settings.

**KOCHANSKI**
But your corrupted files are what make you, you.

**KRYTEN**
I've been diagnosed as being 'quirky' and 'unstable'. Spin my nipple nuts and send me to Alaska - 'quirky'? How could they reach a verdict like that? And as for 'unstable' it makes me so ...

**He pulls a series of bizarre expressions.**

**KRYTEN**
Darn it, I still haven't got the hang of that emotion, have I?

**KOCHANSKI**
What was it supposed to be?

**KRYTEN**
Ambivalence, it didn't come out right though, did it? I looked more like Mr Lister when he's forced to eat fruit.

**KOCHANSKI**
Well, look, what are you going to do?

**KRYTEN**
I have to go along with it, ma'am, I can't say 'no', they are my superiors.

**KOCHANSKI**
No, you've got to say 'no'.

**KRYTEN**
I can't. They're better than me. I'm not strong enough.

**KOCHANSKI**
Right, here's a tip. If you get scared tomorrow, just imagine what they look like on the loo. Can you see them?

**KRYTEN**
No, I - oh, yes, I can.

**Kryten laughs.**

**KOCHANSKI**
Do they still seem better than you?

**KRYTEN**
No, ma'am.

**KOCHANSKI**
Do they still seem superior?

**KRYTEN**
No, ma'am.

**KOCHANSKI**
That's what you've got to do tomorrow. Just re-create that picture.

**Kryten starts laughing.**

**KRYTEN**
It works for everyone.

**KOCHANSKI**
Yes! Who you looking at now?

**KRYTEN**
You, ma'am.

## 10 INT. BOARD OF ENQUIRY ROOM - DAY

~~Lister, Kochanski, Kryten and the Cat all sit.~~

**KOCHANSKI**
I don't want to sound wet, OK ...

**CAT**
Look out moisture alert.

**KOCHANSKI**
I mean, just because I've got a cuddly dinosaur nightie holder and matching pencil case doesn't mean I'm not hard, OK? Because I am hard, in fact, I could have joined the Space Marines if their rules had been different about taking hand cream on manoeuvres. So although I'm hard, and that I think is pretty well established, despite all that hardness, the idea of going to jail (**Falls apart**) God!!!

**LISTER**
Kris, man, it's going to be OK.

**KOCHANSKI**
I'm not going to cope. I'm going to be like that Scots bloke in that prisoner of war film who goes screwy and just bolts for the perimeter fence and starts climbing it. Then rat-a-tat-tat, rat-a-tat-tat, ~~rat a tat tat tat.~~

~~**CAT**~~
He started doing a tap dance? Boy he really must have gone screwy.

**KOCHANSKI**
They shot him!

**CAT**
~~For tapdancing? Nazi bastards!~~

**GUARD**
Be upstanding.

**LISTER**
Just relax. Rimmer's going to help us escape. This enquiry's a piece a cake, we just go through the motions.

**The 3-person board enter.**

**HOLLISTER**
Let's get this enquiry underway. You have refused defence assistance, is that right?

**Cat holds up his hand and they go into a huddle.**

**CAT**
OK, this is what we do, I've watched a lot of TV shows and we all huddle together like this and whisper for a while before we answer. It looks like we know what we're doing.

**They come out of the huddle.**

**CAT**
(**To Hollister**) We intend to defend ourselves.
(**To the gang**) You see how good that looked?

**HOLLISTER**
Are you familiar with the mind scan?

**LISTER**
We are familiar with the mind scan, sir.

**HOLLISTER**
You are aware that it pictorially enhances the cognitive process, making your innermost thoughts available for recording and viewing to a board of enquiry?

**KOCHANSKI**
Yes, sir.

HE STARTED DOING DANCE? BOY HE REA HAVE GONE SCREWY.

KOCHANSKI THEY SHOT HIM!

CAT FOR TAPDANCING? N BASTARDS!

GUARD BE UPSTANDING.

LISTER JUST RELAX. RIMME GOING TO HELP US ENQUIRY'S A CAKE, WE JUST GO THE MOTIONS.

THE 3 PERSON BOAR

HOLLISTER LET'S GET THIS EN UNDERWAY. YOU HAV REFUSED DEFENCE A TANCE, IS THAT RI

CAT HOLDS UP HIS THEY GO INTO A HU

**HOLLISTER**
You understand that it will involve the administration of psychotropic drugs, that is drugs which affect your mental state, making this process possible? If you'll accept say 'Aye'.

**ALL**
Aye.

**HOLLISTER**
Please sign the consent forms and seal them into the envelopes provided. We reconvene at 10am tomorrow.

~~**CAT**~~
~~I'm busy tomorrow, I was hoping to get a manicure and leg wax, how about Thursday?~~

**HOLLISTER**
Tomorrow.

**CAT**
~~OK, but if there's a round where we have to give evidence in swimsuits, I'm out of here.~~

## 11 INT. VISITING AREA - DAY

**Rimmer enters. Lister sits.**

**RIMMER**
The plan's working, Listy. Operation: Get Rimmer Officerhood Power and Eminence. Or G.R.O.P.E. for short - is bang on course.

**LISTER**
So that information I gave you on drive plates worked then, yes-s!

**RIMMER**
The Captain's face, he couldn't have been happier if I'd given him two girls wrestling in a giant vat of baked beans, then removed the girls and handed him a spoon. He's never been so pleased. And get this. He's invited me to supper with the movers and the shakers.

**LISTER**
The movers and the shakers?
You're going to supper with some removal men and a group of people suffering from Parkinson's disease?

**RIMMER**
At last I'll be able to exorcize my father's disapproval. Those terrible sneery looks he used to give me as he stood on the touchline, watching me Captain the school skipping team.

He was never proud of me. What other father would claim to have an alibi for his sperm on the night of conception. But who cares now? Not me, Listy, I'm on my way, up the ziggurat, lickety split.

**LISTER**
Well, don't forget your part of the deal.
The override code for this, so I can leg it.

**Indicates bracelet.**

**RIMMER**
It's too soon. I'm not an officer yet.

**LISTER**
The trial begins tomorrow, man. Without the Nanobots our defence ~~is gonna be as watertight as a supacaver economy cabin on the *Titanic*.~~ has got more holes than my socks.

**RIMMER**
But once you've legged it where does that leave me? I'm not helping you escape and losing all my insider knowledge. I'm not an officer yet.

**LISTER**
Whoowe! We shook hands on a deal.

**RIMMER**
Yeah, but Lister, you know me. My handshake's less reliable than a plumber's estimate.

**LISTER**
No escapo, no more info.

**Rimmer holds up a disc.**

**RIMMER**
Listy, it's not going to help you. I've got the confidential files. Plus I went through Starbug's salvage and I found these.

**He holds up two test-tubes marked 'Luck Virus' and 'Sexual Magnetism'. Lister takes both tubes. Surreptitiously, he wipes his finger down a streak of congealed liquid that's hardened down the Luck Virus. Rimmer takes it off him.**

**LISTER**
'Luck Virus', 'Sexual Magnetism'.

**RIMMER**
Positive viruses. Holly told me everything. Take some of this - it gives you luck and this gives you sexual magnetism. I've already tried some. Right now Yvonne McGruder is sleeping off the first twenty-three pages of the *Kama Sutra*.

**LISTER**
So you're reneging on the deal, then. Breaking your promise. Being a total scum-sucking, two-faced weaselly weasel?

**RIMMER**
Ah, my entry in *Who's Who*.

Rimmer exits. Lister gives him the finger. Then he licks his finger.

**LISTER**
You left some of your luck behind, man. I touched the tube.

He types the override code into his restraint harness. It unclicks.

**LISTER**
Sheer luck.

Lister punches in code. Door opens.

**LISTER**
Yes!

## 12 INT. OLD DENTIST SET - DAY

A 4-person panel: Doc Newton, Panel Woman Officer, Extra Officer, and MP Thornton, stands by.

**PANEL WOMAN OFFICER**
You may, if you prefer, stand with the others tomorrow and face the charges against you. However, I advise that you have your corrupted files repaired, after which you may go free. What is your decision?

**KRYTEN**
Nnnn - nnn - nnn - nnn - nnn. NNNN. NNNNNNNNNNNN. Oh, it's no good.

Kryten grabs MP Thornton's gun out of his holster and points it at them.

**THERAPIST**
OK, let's all stay calm, no need to be alarmed. After all, Kryten is merely holding us hostage, which is lovely, isn't it everyone?

**DOC NEWTON**
We don't want any trouble, we'll do just what you say.

**KRYTEN**
Come on then. Come with me.

## 13 INT. TOILETS - DAY

MP Thornton, Doc Newton, Panel Woman Officer, Therapist and Extra Officer enter the toilets. Kryten still pointing the gun.

**KRYTEN**
Now, I want you to take down your pants and sit on a toilet.

**PANEL WOMAN OFFICER**
Oh, my God, he's mad.

**DOC NEWTON**
Then what are you going to do to us?

**KRYTEN**
I'm going to look at you.

**PANEL WOMAN OFFICER**
He's totally mad.

**DOC NEWTON**
Just do what he says.

**THERAPIST**
Lovely.

They all take their pants down and sit on the toilets, the doors open. Kryten walks from cubicle to cubicle peering in and laughing. Finally he gathers himself.

**KRYTEN**
Now, I want you to ask me the question again.

**PANEL WOMAN OFFICER**
What question?

**KRYTEN**
Do I want to have my corrupted files repaired?

**DOC NEWTON**
Do you want to have your corrupted files repaired?

**KRYTEN**
Nnnnnnnnnn. Nnnnnnnnnnn. No. I did it. No. Nnnnn-no, I don't. The answer to the question is 'no'. No doubt about it, I do not want to have my corrupted files repaired. The answer is nnnn 'no'.

Kryten laughs triumphantly.
Two guards come in, grab him and inject him with something.

14 INT. ANOTHER CORRIDOR – DAY

Lister, in makeshift disguise, and Kochanski, also disguised, walk along a corridor. They step into a lift.

15 MODEL SEQUENCE
Lift hammers down vent.

16 INT. LIFT – DAY

**KOCHANSKI**
And you just put in any old code you felt like and the Luck Virus made you pick the right one. It's brilliant.

**LISTER**
Yeah! Just rubbed my finger on the top of the tube.

**KOCHANSKI**
That's brilliant, that's just brilliant. It's a pity you didn't do the same with the Sexual Magnetism. (**Laughs**)

Lister's eyes widen. He did touch the tube with Sexual Magnetism in it. He licks his left hand forefinger.

Kochanski smiles at him. He smiles back.

**KOCHANSKI**
Is that a new shirt?

**LISTER**
No, I've had it a while.

**KOCHANSKI**
Oh, it's really nice.

**LISTER**
Thanks.

**KOCHANSKI**
It's really, really nice. Really suits you.

**LISTER**
Thanks.

**KOCHANSKI**
Brings out the brownness in your eyes.

She grabs him and snogs him big time, then starts tearing off his clothes. Suddenly she stops.

**KOCHANSKI**
Oh, God, Dave, I'm so sorry - I don't know what happened there.

**LISTER**
I think I do. I had some Sexual Magnetism Virus on this hand but the Luck Virus cured it for me.

Talks to his right index finger.

**LISTER**
Thanks, pal.

**KOCHANSKI**
I don't know what got into me.

**LISTER**
Well, nothing sadly.

## 17 INT. MEDI-BAY - COMPUTER GRAPHIC SEQUENCE

**Kryten is plugged into a computer worked by the Panel Woman Officer.**

On screen:

**Robert Llewellyn appears like the Doctor off 'Norton Utilities'. (We'll affect him somehow to make him look computerized - Max Headroomy?)**

**DATA DOCTOR** (Robert Llewellyn)
Hello, I'm the Data Doctor, if you would like me to examine your hard disc press 'examine'.

**The examine button is clicked.**

**DATA DOCTOR** (Robert Llewellyn)
Your mechanoid appears to have developed the following rogue emotions: affection, arrogance, envy, guilt, humour, insecurity, petulance, possessiveness, snobbery, and love. If you wish to eradicate these emotions from his database press 'fix'.

**The mouse pointer clicks 'fix'.**

**All the different emotions flash up on the screen and are fixed.**

**Montage of the word 'Fixed' appears on screen. All shapes and sizes.**

**DATA DOCTOR** (Robert Llewellyn)
All bad line blocks and corrupted personality discs have now been fixed. Please reboot your mechanoid - his personality has now been restored to its factory settings.

**On screen the pointer presses reboot.**

**KRYTEN**
My name is Kryten, I'm programmed to serve. Can I be of service?

**Kryten stands and has a stifled robotic walk.**

**PANEL WOMAN OFFICER**
Bring me a coffee, please, Kryten.

**KRYTEN**
Certainly, ma'am.

**PANEL WOMAN OFFICER**
Then you may scrub the floor.

**KRYTEN**
Yes, ma'am.

**PANEL WOMAN OFFICER**
Are you happy, Kryten?

**KRYTEN**
I have no understanding of human emotions, ma'am. I am programmed to serve.

**PANEL WOMAN OFFICER**
Excellent.

## 18 INT. CORRIDOR - DAY

**Rimmer makes his way to the Captain's supper. He brushes down his jacket, then takes out the 'Sexual Magnetism' Virus and swigs.**

**RIMMER**
I'm going to be Colin Charisma at the Captain's supper with this stuff.

**He walks along, girls say 'hi', flirtatiously.**

## 19 INT. CAPTAIN'S QUARTERS - EVENING

**Hollister is entertaining the chosen.**

Captain Frank Hollister
Requests the pleasure of your company
For Supper, In the Captain's Quarters
This coming Friday.

R.S.V.P

**RIMMER**
And if we approach light speed I think we have to be aware we could come across something I believe we'll experience called 'Future Echoes', episodal pockets of futurey things from the future.

**DOC NEWTON**
How fascinating. What a fascinating man you are, Mr Rimmer.

**HOLLISTER**
I think we've greatly underestimated you over the years, Arnold. Now, let me find out where that coffee is.

**DOC NEWTON**
Oh, no, Captain, please - allow me.

**She gets up.**

**DOC NEWTON**
Perhaps you could help me, Mr Rimmer?

**RIMMER**
Why certainly, and perhaps we can talk about my theory on backwards universes.

**They walk out of the room.**

## 20 INT. CORRIDOR OUTSIDE CAPTAIN'S QUARTERS - EVENING

**RIMMER**
... and of course in a backwards universe many things start to make more sense ...

**She grabs him and snogs him.**

**DOC NEWTON**
Oh, my God, you are sexy. So very, very sexy.

**She pushes him roughly into a room marked kitchen. There is the sound of a lot of crashing pots and pans.**

## 21 CGI/MODEL SEQUENCE

**Lift hammers down shaft.**

## 22 INT. LIFT - EVENING

**Cat, Kochanski and Lister.**

**CAT**
Bravo, bud. What now?

**LISTER**
Well, we find Kryten, get to the Landing Bay, grab a ship and get the hell out of town. He's on this floor.

Lister, Kochanski and Cat exit lift into:-

## 23 INT. CORRIDOR OUTSIDE DENTIST'S - EVENING

Lister, Kochanski and Cat.

**LISTER**
Here he is. Krytie, come on.

**KRYTEN**
(English Butler accent) Are you addressing me, sir? I don't believe we've had the pleasure?

**LISTER**
What have they done to you, Kryten? You sound like Noel Coward's elocution teacher.

**KRYTEN**
Well, if you'll forgive me, sir, I have my duties to perform. Good day.

**KOCHANSKI**
They've fixed all his corrupted files. He musn't have been able to say 'no'. Someone's coming.

**LISTER**
We've gotta get a better disguise.

**CAT**
We've already got a disguise.

**LISTER**
What's the point of a disguise if you wear it under your normal outfit?

**CAT**
A grey boiler suit?! You think I'm going to wear this on the outside?

They exit into:

## 24 INT. DENTIST'S - DAY

**LISTER**
Look, we're not leaving without him. I don't care what they've done to him, he's coming with us, he's part of the posse.

Cat opens a broom cupboard with some mops in it. He looks through various false teeth.

**CAT**
Hey, I've got a great idea for a new disguise.

**LISTER**
What?

Cat turns wearing teeth and mop head.

**CAT**
The Dibbley family.

**LISTER/KOCHANSKI**
Yes!

Lister and Kochanski also dress and turn to face camera.

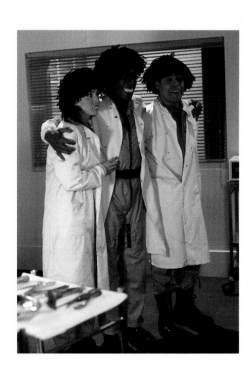

## 25 INT. CAPTAIN'S QUARTERS - EVENING

Rimmer and Doc Newton return looking slightly flustered.

**HOLLISTER**
Ah, there you are. Any news on the coffee?

**RIMMER**
Drat, we forgot. I'll find out right away, sir.

**SECOND WOMAN OFFICER**
I'll give you a hand, Mr Rimmer.

A largish, middle-aged, matronly type gets up and follows him.

## 26 INT. CORRIDOR - EVENING

Hard cut to outside the kitchen where we see Second Woman Officer and Rimmer through porthole.

## 27 INT. DENTIST'S - DAY

Lister, Kochanski and the Cat are now wearing the mop heads with Dibbley teeth and white dentist coats. The door opens. Thornton and fellow guard enter.

**MP THORNTON**
Sorry to interrupt, sir, but we're searching this floor for the escaped prisoners.

**CAT/DUANE**
Sorry, we haven't seen them. There's just me, my wife here and my brother.

**LISTER**
(Dib voice) Hello.

**KOCHANSKI**
(Dib voice) Hi.

**LISTER**
(Dib voice) Hi.

**MP THORNTON**
I don't recollect seeing you guys before.

**CAT/DUANE**
That's because we don't go out much looking like this.

**MP THORNTON**
What do you guys do?

**DIBBLEYS**
(They look at one another - what else could it be?) Computer programmers.

**MP THORNTON**
Well, if you see anything suspicious, call security, OK?

**KOCHANSKI**
(Dib voice) You bet.

Kryten enters as the guards get set to leave.

**KRYTEN**
(English accent) Begging your pardons, sirs, I just need to get a mop.

Goes over to cupboard.

**KRYTEN**
How peculiar, my mop heads are missing.

3 shot - Dibbley family look nervy.

**KRYTEN**
Don't I know you, sir? Wayne. Wayne something ... Wayne ... Wibbley. Where do I know you from?

**CAT/DUANE**
(Dib Voice) No, no, no, sir, you're mistaken. You're mixing me up with some other big-teethed dork.

**LISTER**
(Dib Voice) No, let him speak ... Where do you know him from?

52

**CAT**
(**Dib Voice**) Are you out of your mind?

**LISTER**
(**Dib Voice**) Where do you know him from? Think.

**KRYTEN**
I feel I'm about to discover something wonderful, but when I discover it, it will put someone in great danger. I feel an emotion, I feel two emotions, two different emotions. I feel ... I feel ...

**KOCHANSKI**
(**Dib Voice**) ... ambivalence.

**KRYTEN**
I can feel my files corrupting. They're corrupting. (**Normal accent**) Oh, yes, that's good ...

The guards stand watching. Kryten's face indicates he's going through a series of strange emotions.

**KRYTEN**
I'm back. And I'm baaaad. Obviously within certain sensible preset parameters.

**TANNOY V/O**
Attention, attention. Reported prisoner sighting on C Deck, reported prisoner sighting on C Deck.

Guards exit. Kochanski frowns.

**LISTER**
Nice one, Hol. (**Pause. To Kochanski**) What's wrong with you?

**KOCHANSKI**
Well, do you get the impression this is too easy? Like everything's going for us. Like they almost want us to escape.

Lister gives her the finger.

**KOCHANSKI**
Hey, I was just thinking aloud.

**LISTER**
No, no, the Luck Virus, it's helping us.

Lister takes off wig and sneezes into it.
Puts it back on his head.

**LISTER**
(**Points to Kryten**) Put your kit on.

## 28 INT. CAPTAIN'S QUARTERS – EVENING

~~Hollister looks at his watch as a large pair of pants drifts past the window behind him.~~

Rimmer and Second Woman Officer enter looking dishevelled.

**RIMMER**
Here we are, remembered the coffee at last.

**HOLLISTER**
What about the mints?

**LAST WOMAN OFFICER**
I'll go. Would you like to help me, Mr Rimmer.

**RIMMER**
(**Plaintiff**) It's just I've got so much coffee, I don't think I can manage to get any mints until tomorrow.

Last Woman Officer exits for mints by herself.

**HOLLISTER**
Well, the psychotropic testing should be well under way by now. Those results sure are going to be interesting.

**RIMMER**
Psychotropic what?

**HOLLISTER**
The Lister case is so unusual that I've decided to invoke my right to use psychotropic evidence. The accused are drugged, wired to a mainframe, then the computer feeds in various hypothetical scenarios and their reactions are laid down on tape. Right now, they believe they're escaping but we just want to observe what they do.

**RIMMER**
So that means that if anyone happens to mention any special agreements that they entered into - then ... could you excuse me - I think I've left the iron on.

## 29 INT. CORRIDOR OUTSIDE CAPTAIN'S QUARTERS - EVENING

Rimmer rushes out into the corridor. More women say 'Hi'. He's tempted.

**RIMMER**
Hi! What is wrong with me? I've got the sexual appetite of a mountain lion, no, worse, a first year nursing student. It's just being wanted, it's such an aphrodisiac. Got to get some control back.

Rimmer enters dentist's office.

## 30 INT. DENTIST'S OFFICE - EVENING

He injects his groin with a local anaesthetic. Punches himself in the balls with a mallet. No pain. He smiles and exits.

## 31 INT. CORRIDOR OUTSIDE CAPTAIN'S QUARTERS - EVENING

Rimmer starts to walk down the corridor but the anaesthetic starts to spread to his legs. He starts to walk most strangely as the top half of his legs go to sleep. He passes some women and they all say 'hi'. He passes the Captain on his way to loo.

**HOLLISTER**
Never realised you were so damn popular with the ladies. Maybe you can share your secret sometime.

**RIMMER**
Yes, sir.

Rimmer continues doing his funny walk. Hollister watches him baffled.

## 32 INT. CORRIDOR - DAY

The Dibbley family including Dibbley Kryten enter shot like the guys from *Reservoir Dogs*.
Two Skutters pass. They do a double take, swing round and start following them, making the Skutter whistle noise to attract attention.

**LISTER**
Guys, it's Bob and Madge. Go on, shoo, guys. Shoo, go on. We're trying to escape.

The Skutter makes a Skuttery noise.

**LISTER**
You'll never get past security, go on, on.

The Skutters go into the dentists and re-emerge wearing Dibbley disguises of their own - hair and teeth.
They start following Lister and co.

CAPTION: 'TO BE CONTINUED'.

## TITLES

FADE TO BLACK

# BACKINTHERED
## PART TWO.

## *Cast & Crew*

Written by: **DOUG** NAYLOR

Rimmer: **CHRIS** BARRIE  Lister: **CRAIG** CHARLES  Cat: **DANNY** JOHN-JULES

Kryten: **ROBERT** LLEWELLYN  Kochanski: **CHLOË** ANNETT  Holly: **NORMAN** LOVETT

Hollister: **MAC** McDONALD  Doc Newton: **KIKA** MIRYLEES

Panel Woman Officer: **JEMMA** CHURCHILL  Dr McClaren: **ANDY** TAYLOR

Second Woman Officer: **SUE** KELVIN  MP Thornton: **KARL** GLENN STIMPSON

Last Woman Officer: **GENEVIEVE** SWALLOW  Doctor: **GEOFFREY** BEEVERS


Casting Director: **LINDA** GLOVER  Music: **HOWARD** GOODALL

Production Accountant: **MIKE** AMOS  Graphic Designer: **ANDY** SPENCE  **BEN** SHEPHERD

General Manager GNP LTD: **HELEN** NORMAN  Production Co-ordinator: **RACHEL** STEWART

Post-Production Co-ordinator: **SIMON** BURCHELL

Stage Manager: **JACQUELINE** ZOPPI-TIGHE  Gaffer: **JOHN** BARKER

Props Master: **PAUL** DE CSERNATONY  Props Buyer: **TIM** YOUNGMAN

Art Director: **IAN** READE-HILL  Vision Mixer: **JOHN** BARCLAY

Engineering Manager: **ALAN** GODLEMAN  Camera Operator: **ANDY** MARTIN

Location Sound: **NIGEL** DAVIS  Sound Supervisor: **JEM** WHIPPEY  **Geoff** Moss

Editor: **MARK** WYBOURN  Script Associate: **PAUL** ALEXANDER

Script Supervisor: **GILLIAN** WOOD  First Assistant Director: **JULIE** SYKES

Visual Effects Designer: **JIM** FRANCIS  **Bill** Pearson  **Mark** Howard

Digital Effects Designer: **CHRIS** VEALE  Make Up Designer: **ANDREA** FINCH

Costume Designer: **HOWARD** BURDEN  Line Producer: **JO** BENNETT

Production Designer: **MEL** BIBBY  Director of Photography: **PETER** MORGAN

Executive Producer: **DOUG** NAYLOR  Produced and Directed by: **ED** BYE

One of the hardest sequences we've ever had to shoot on Red Dwarf was the Cat tap dance sequence with Blue Midget.

Just writing that last sentence has brought me out in a cold sweat.

In all, the sequence lasted about two minutes of screen time, but took three months of planning to shoot. Which in TV terms is an eternity.

The first stage was storyboarding.

For eight, five-hour meetings, Ed, Chris and I had talked the sequence through in the minutest detail before Chris went off and did several drafts onto storyboard, breaking the sequence down, shot by shot.

A Blue Midget miniature had been constructed for the re-mastered series. Mike Vaughan, the Red Dwarf photographer then came in and shot the miniature Midget from every conceivable angle.

One day.

Once the shots were developed, Chris Veale then scanned them into his computer, constructed a wire-frame model of the ship and started to add the textures taken from the photographs.

Ten days.

We needed a choreographer. One whom Danny trusted and ideally one who knew something about blue screen.

Six meetings, talking to various choreographers. Finally ...

Step aboard Charles Augins, whom we all knew from working together on 'Queeg', where he'd played the title role. As well as acting, Charles had been a choreographer for many years and had worked with Danny on countless occasions.

Chris Veale appeared and explained he wanted to shoot Danny dancing first and then add the dancing Blue Midgets. The idea being he would programme his computer to get the Midgets to mimic Danny's steps.

Four meetings.

We needed some music.

Ten meetings, different pieces are commissioned and rejected before we find a piece everyone is happy with.

The music in place, we start to shoot.

We shoot Danny first, in a set which consists of a blue floor and three blue walls.

Ed's brain starts leaking as he works out what Danny's eyelines have to be and where he should be standing in relation to five giant Blue Midgets which aren't there and obviously haven't been added yet.

This takes several twelve-hour days.

The Floor Manager later confesses that none of the crew or anyone on set had the slightest idea what Ed and Peter Morgan, the lighting camera-man, were doing, why they were doing it and how the whole crew think this is going to be a disaster.

I start to think what everyone has been thinking for some time - why didn't I just write a scene with some funny dialogue?

Finally, finally, finally, the shoot is completed.

Chris Veale takes away an edited version of the dance on blue screen and Peter Morgan the lighting cameraman then lights and shoots a series of stills from the miniature Landing Bay we used for the Starbug crash from 'Back in the Red - Pt 1' so Chris can use them as his background plates when he comes to build the set for the sequence in his computer.

Several days.

Chris creates the Midgets.

More days.

Adds the plates.

More days.

Adds Danny.

More days.

We cut the sequence together. Ed and I then go over to Chris's house and decide we want to drop most of the CGI backgrounds, created in Chris's computer, and substitute them with Peter Morgan's miniature plates because they look more realistic.

More shots are made, another edit.

More days.

And then another and then another.

More days.

Mark Wybourn, the VT editor, then traces around the dancing teeth, turns the image black and angles it on the shot to make it look like a drop shadow. This makes the teeth look like they really are on the floor and not a pair of choppers that are operated by a blue rod, which is what they were.

Mark also takes the Ground Controller's exploding booth shot and multiplies it exponentially to give the impression that there were twenty or so Ground Controllers and then takes glass fragments and mixes them onto the sixteen different explosion shots.

More days.

Finally, finally, finally the sequence is complete. The show is broadcast.

Someone tells me people on the Red Dwarf newsgroup hate it.

Literally thousands and thousands of hours of work and they hate it.

One member of the newsgroup says we just did the dance to pad out the show.

Pad out the show?

Aaaaaagggggghhhhhhhh!!!!!!

# RED DWARF VIII

## 'BACK IN THE RED - PART 3'

### EPISODE 3

## Written by
## DOUG NAYLOR

DANCE NO LATERAL MOVE-
MENT, HEAD TO TOE. BLUE
MIDGET COPIES.

2 shot Cat and Blue
Midget - Cat and Blue
Midget kick off a duet
DUANE DOES SECOND MAD
they do identical slick
DUANE DANCE, SIMILAR
dance steps for 8 bars
or so. SHOTS see TO PREVIOUS,
ter with the steps. Cat
WHICH BLUE MIDGET
kicks them across the
COPIES AND THEN TOPS.
cargo bay.

WHEN IT FINISHES IT
Cat and Blue Midget
dance. TURNS TO LOOK BACK AT
Midget DUANNE, SPOTLIGHTING
kicks Cat out of shot.
HIM.

41 INT. GROUND CONTROL
-DUANE DOES MAD DUANE shot Ground CLOSE UP DUANE

CASTANETS. Cat and Blue Midget dance. Cat kicks Blue Midget. Blue Midget kicks Cat ou
s 2 shot Cat and Blue Midget - Cat and Blue Midget ki
Mid off a duet, they do identical slick dance steps for
shot Ground Control
Cat walks up to Blue Midget. The six Blue Midgets and the Cat start to do
9 INT. GROUND CONTROL.
bars or so. The teeth chatter with the steps. Cat ki
Montage of shots as window after window in the Ground Controller's control ba
AY
is them across the cargo ba
Cat and Blue Midget dance. Cat kicks Blue Midget. HI
with shatt
SHOT OF GROUND CON-
The Vibrati
Multiple mid shots of Midget kicks Cat out of sho
TROLLER. NOT AMUSED.
Mid shot Ground Controlle
Cat walks up to Blue Midget. The six Blue Midgets a
the Cat start to do big stompy dance numbe
0 INT. CARGO BAY. DAY
Montage of shots as window after window in the Grou
Controller's Control room is shatter
CAT THROWS THE TEETH
with the vibration
OUT OF SHOT. THEY START
Multiple mid shots
CHATTERING ON THE

# BACKINTHERED
## PART THREE.

### TITLES

**1 INT. CGI SHOT**

**Prison establisher**

**2 INT. PRISON QUARTERS –
DAY**

**Rimmer and Lister in lilac enter, their first day
over. Rimmer looks around.**

**RIMMER**
One day in this lousy stinking Penal Colony and
I'm cracking up. Everyone's so deranged and
brutal, it's frightening. This afternoon, I was so
depressed, I went to see the social worker.

**LISTER**
Was he any help?

**RIMMER**
Not really, he beat me up. He said I was a
whining nancy boy with girlie white legs.
Then pummelled me repeatedly with his
book: *Showing Compassion to Inmates.*

**LISTER**
I thought social workers were supposed to
be nice?

**RIMMER**
So did I. I also thought they were supposed to
wear corduroy jackets with leather patches and
drive Volvos. But this guy didn't, I don't reckon
he was fully qualified. In the end, I was so shell
shocked, I went to see the Priest, and explained
everything.

**LISTER**
What did he say?

**RIMMER**
He said I was a whining baby who was missing
his mum, then he beat me up too. You can still
see crucifix marks in the back of my head.

**LISTER**
It's because we're in G Tower, all the staff are
mad here. One of the guys was saying though, as
a reward for good behaviour, they move you to
the luxury block on D wing. Everything's really
nice there. Even shampoo the rats. Groom their
tails and everything.

**RIMMER**
I must look it up in my Michelin Guide to Penal
Colony hell holes, I'm sure it probably gets the
full five slop-out buckets.

**LISTER**
They've got everything. TVs, music centres,
they've even got a trouser press.

**RIMMER**
Since when were you interested in a trouser
press? You care less about your appearance
than a member of the Dutch royal family.

**LISTER**
No, I was thinking if we got moved to a cell with
a trouser press, we could make cheese toasties.

**Rimmer picks up envelope from desk and takes out
a leaflet.**

**RIMMER**
What's this?

**He picks up leaflet.**

**RIMMER**
(**Reads**) 'Floor 13 - Information Pack. If privacy
is required when using toilet, please wear
blindfold.'

**Rimmer pulls blindfold out of envelope.**

**LISTER**
What's the book?

**RIMMER**
Gideon's *Bible*.

**LISTER**
He follows me everywhere that bloke. I stayed in a hotel once, he left his bible behind there as well. Then two years later, another hotel, and the dozy git had left it behind again.

**RIMMER**
(Sigh) Everything is ruined, my career is over, I've no goal, no hope, no life.

**LISTER**
Yeah, but how come that's started getting you down now?

**RIMMER**
Maybe you haven't noticed but we are going to spend the next two years in the brig. Two years with the scum of the universe, hardened criminals, deranged droids, people so unbalanced and debauched they couldn't even get elected as President of the United States. We've got to escape.

**LISTER**
No, there's security cameras everywhere. Y'know that mad geezer with one eye and the funny tic, he said it was impossible.

**RIMMER**
Well, he's bound to say that - he's the warden. If only I'd hired a smarter lawyer. Instead of the brain-dead, pompous, stupid-haired git I ended up with.

**LISTER**
You defended yourself.

**RIMMER**
Yes, and I don't need reminding of that, thank you very much. Two years in the Tank!

**LISTER**
Two years.

Rimmer puts blindfold on.

**RIMMER**
How did I get into this mess?

**LISTER**
I think the blindfold is supposed to be for me.

## 3 CGI/MODEL SEQUENCE
Red Dwarf in space.

Text:- 2 days earlier.

## 4 INT. HOLLISTER'S OFFICE - DAY
Hollister speaks into a camera - captain's log type.

**HOLLISTER**
This is a diary of Captain F. Hollister of the mining ship Red Dwarf. Several of my crew are presently being tried for crimes against the Space Corps.

## 5 INT. BOARD OF ENQUIRY - DAY (RECAP)
Board of enquiry (Hollister and 2x women) of Lister, Cat, Kryten and Kochanski (sitting opposite them).

**HOLLISTER**
Are you familiar with the mind scan?

**LISTER**
We are familiar with the mind scan, sir.

**HOLLISTER**
You understand that it will involve the administration of psychotropic drugs, that is drugs which affect your mental state, making this process possible? If you'll accept say 'Aye'.

**ALL**
Aye.

**HOLLISTER**
Please sign the consent forms and seal them into the envelopes provided. We reconvene at 10am tomorrow.

## 6 INT. HOLLISTER'S OFFICE - DAY

To camera - as before.

**HOLLISTER**
To test the veracity of their defence, unknown to them, I've had them placed in artificial reality where their actions can be observed.

## 7 INT. AR SUITE - DAY (RECAP)

**Posse in AR. We see recap - all of them dressed as Dibbleys walking down corridor to music.**

**Cut to:-**

## 8 INT. CAPTAIN'S QUARTERS - EVENING (RECAP)

**Hollister and others sitting round table having candle lit supper.**

**HOLLISTER**
(To Rimmer) ... Right now, they believe they're escaping but we just want to observe what they do.

**RIMMER**
So that means, that if anyone happens to mention any special agreements that they entered into ... could you excuse me - I think I've left the iron on.

## 9 INT. HOLLISTER'S OFFICE - DAY

To camera - as before.

**HOLLISTER**
Rimmer, one of the least able of my crew.

## 10 INT. HOLLISTER'S OFFICE - DAY (RECAP)

**Rimmer doing extra long salute then limping off.**

## 11 INT. HOLLISTER'S OFFICE - DAY

To camera - as before.

**HOLLISTER**
... has started acting very suspiciously, being incredibly insightful and efficient.

## 12 INT. HOLLISTER'S OFFICE - DAY (RECAP)

**Rimmer puts report on Hollister's desk.**

## 13 INT. HOLLISTER'S OFFICE - DAY

To camera - as before.

**HOLLISTER**
I suspect he may have access to the crew's confidential files. We also believe he may be in possession of a virus which makes him incredibly attractive to the opposite sex. This is obviously a remarkable serum and as a responsible senior officer of the Space Corps, it's imperative I gain possession of this solution and use some myself.

## 14 INT. CORRIDOR OUTSIDE CAPTAIN'S QUARTERS - EVENING (RECAP)

**Rimmer and female officer - Doc. Newton, holding each other.**

**DOC NEWTON**
Oh, my God, you are sexy. So very, very sexy.

**She pushes him roughly into a room marked kitchen.**

## 15 INT. HOLLISTER'S OFFICE - DAY

To camera - as before.

**HOLLISTER**
Yesterday he was observed injecting his groin with anaesthetic, something we believe he did to regain some self-control.

## 16 INT MEDI-BAY - DAY (RECAP)

**Rimmer injects his groin with anaesthetic.**

## 17 INT. CORRIDOR - DAY (RECAP)

**Rimmer gets funny walk. He passes a group of girls.**

**RIMMER**
Hi.

**GIRLS**
(Lustfully) Hi!

## 18 INT. HOLLISTER'S OFFICE - DAY

To camera - as before.

**HOLLISTER**
I also suspect someone, possibly Lister, has given Rimmer access to the crew's confidential files and he's using this information to blackmail his way up the chain of command. It's sickening, it's unforgivable but it's a technique that can work. I should know, I used the same method myself to become Captain. If the crew discover I'm really just Dennis the Doughnut Boy - I'm finished. I will continue to observe Lister's actions in AR, and expect my suspicions to be confirmed. Report ends.

## 19 INT. AR AREA - DAY

Lister, Kryten, Cat and Kochanski stand in the AR machines. Above them on a monitor we see:-

## 20 EXT/INT. LANDING BAY - DAY

Cat/Duane walks, pushing a laundry basket with crew in, and starts to board Blue Midget. Duane Skutters follow.

## 21 INT. BLUE MIDGET - DAY

Lister et al get out of laundry basket and hide out of view. Dibbley Skutters come aboard too.

Cat sits in the pilot seat and starts to flick switches which turn on the retros. The scannner blinks on and ...

## 22 INT. GROUND CONTROL - DAY

**GROUND CONTROL**
This is Ground Control to Midget 3, you don't appear to have flight clearance. Please state your name and clearance code.

## 23 INT. BLUE MIDGET - DAY

**CAT**
Ground Control this is uh ... uh ...

**LISTER**
Major Tom

**CAT**
... yeah, Major Tom -

## 24 INT. GROUND CONTROL - DAY

**GROUND CONTROL**
Major Tom, what is your clearance code and pilot number?

## 25 INT. BLUE MIDGET - DAY

**CAT**
I'm sorry, I left all my details in my other pants.

## 26 INT. GROUND CONTROL - DAY

**GROUND CONTROL**
I'm sorry, I didn't catch that.

Ground Control comes up on the screen.

### 27 INT. BLUE MIDGET - DAY

Cat/Duane stares at her besotted.

**CAT**
Wow.

### 28 INT. GROUND CONTROL - DAY

**GROUND CONTROL**
Without take-off clearance, I can't permit you to fly.

### 29 INT. BLUE MIDGET - DAY

**CAT**
I can handle this thing, OK? I'm good, I'm better than good - I'm smooth with a capital smoo.

### 30 INT. GROUND CONTROL - DAY

**GROUND CONTROL**
(**Laughs**) Well, that's as maybe but I need a little proof that you can fly that thing.

### 31 INT. BLUE MIDGET - DAY

**CAT**
Fly? I can make this thing dance.

### 32 INT. GROUND CONTROL - DAY

Shot of Ground Controller.

### 33 INT. BLUE MIDGET - DAY

Mid shot Duane with foreground controls - he starts to hit buttons all over the place.

We hear SFX of roof opening.

### 34 INT. CARGO BAY - DAY

Low angle wide as Blue Midget rises to it's feet.

### 35 INT. BLUE MIDGET - REACTION SHOTS TO CAT

Cat stands up. Picks up a metal tea tray and exits.

### 36 INT. CARGO BAY - DAY

Medium shot of 'real' Blue Midget leg built in green and later inlaid into CGI Blue Midget - Duane slides on his tray down the leg and out of shot. Tray clangs onto floor.

### 37 INT. GROUND CONTROL - DAY

Controller looks alarmed.

### 38 INT. CARGO BAY - DAY

Cat walks into 2 shot with Blue Midget. Blue Midget sort of watches him with its headlights, thus follow spotting him.

Duane does mad Duane dance, no lateral movement, head to toe. Blue Midget copies.

Duane does second mad Duane dance, similar shots to previous, which Blue Midget copies and then tops. When it finishes it turns to look back at Duane, spotlighting him.

Medium close up Duane - Duane reacts.

Duane pulls out his Duane teeth and mop head, rips off his clothes and changes into the Cat.We hear a Cat yowl O.O.V. he holds teeth like castanets.

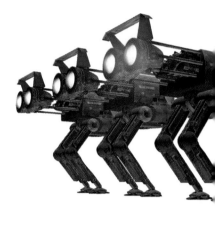

### 39 INT. GROUND CONTROL - DAY

Shot of Ground Controller, not amused.

### 40 INT. CARGO BAY - DAY

Cat throws the teeth out of shot. They start chattering on the ground.

2 shot Cat and Blue Midget - Cat and Blue Midget kick off a duet, they do identical slick dance steps for 8 bars or so. The teeth chatter with the steps. Cat kicks them across the cargo bay.

Cat and Blue Midget dance. Cat kicks Blue Midget. Blue Midget kicks Cat out of shot.

### 41 INT. GROUND CONTROL - DAY

Mid shot Ground Controller.

### 42 INT. CARGO BAY - DAY

Cat walks up to Blue Midget. The six Blue Midgets and the Cat start to do big stompy dance number.

### 43 EXT. GROUND CONTROL - DAY

Montage of shots as window after window in the Ground Controller's control room is shattered with the vibrations.

Multiple mid shots of different Ground Controllers - trying to work out how he's doing it.

### 44 INT. CARGO BAY - DAY

Music builds. High angle wide shot. Dancing.

Full tilt blasting music, they spin, high kicks, jumps.

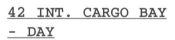

~~The Midgets swivel, facing away from us, pointing their rears in the air and firing off their retros, in time to the music.~~

Little arms come out of the side of all the Blue Midgets and as the music reaches an electric guitar climax all the Midgets air guitar their way to the finish.

### 45 INT. GROUND CONTROL - DAY

Mid shot Ground Controller - totally charmed.

### 46 INT. CARGO BAY - DAY

The Cat jumps onto the first Blue Midget's foot. and is propelled up and out of shot.

Wide shot. Cat sails through the air.

### 47 INT. BLUE MIDGET - DAY

Cat lands in his seat and grins. Music ends.

### 48 INT. GROUND CONTROL - DAY

**GROUND CONTROL**
Wow.

### 49 INT. BLUE MIDGET - DAY

**Cat with a cigar.**

**CAT**
You free Saturday?

### 50 INT. GROUND CONTROL - DAY

**GROUND CONTROL**
I am now.

### 51 INT. BLUE MIDGET - DAY

**CAT**
Holy schmoly - I got a date in three days' time, I better start getting ready.

**LISTER**
You're going nowhere, man, we are out of here.

### 52 INT. CGI SEQUENCE. LANDING BAY. - DAY

**Blue Midget runs along landing bay and takes off.**

### 53 EXT. CGI SEQUENCE

**Blue Midget in space flying from Red Dwarf.**

### 54 INT. CORRIDOR OUTSIDE AR SUITE - DAY

**MP Thornton stands outside. Rimmer approaches, he still has his funny anaesthetised walk.**

**RIMMER**
Thornton.

**MP THORNTON**
No-one's allowed in there Rimmer - beat it.

**RIMMER**
Angus Thornton. Aged 36. Middle name Lionel. Inside leg measurement 29. Neck size 16. Circumcised.

**MP THORNTON**
How do you know all this?

**RIMMER**
Jazz fan, good credit rating, once admitted to hospital totally naked and attached to ...
(**Whispers**)

**MP THORNTON**
That's a vicious, slanderous, filthy stinking

slanderous lie that you just made up.
(**Beat**) Who told you?

**RIMMER**
Want all the crew to know? Take a cigarette break. Five minutes.

**MP THORNTON**
OK, I'm going OK, I'm lighting up already. I'm going.

**Thornton hurries off.**

**Rimmer enters the AR suite.**

### 55 EXT. CGI SEQUENCE

**Blue Midget flying through space.**

### 56 INT. BLUE MIDGET - DAY

**Lister, Kochanski, Kryten and the Cat, driving.**

**LISTER**
Now all we've gotta do is get a bearing on those damn Nanos and we're cruising down freedom boulevard.

### 57 INT. AR SUITE - DAY

**Rimmer watches.**

### 58 INT. AR SUITE/BLUE MIDGET - DAY

**KRYTEN**
Getting something now, sir.

**LISTER**
Good, we didn't need that confidential files scam I cooked up with Rimmer after all, all that stuff I gave him on the Captain. The double-dealing, two-faced rat.

## 59 INT. AR SUITE - DAY

**Rimmer looks at a computery type machine which is recording everything.**

**He starts to type.**

**RIMMER**
(Typing) Find all references to the agreement between Lister and Rimmer and remove.

**He presses a button.**

**MACHINE V/O:- All references removed.**

## 60 INT. BLUE MIDGET - DAY

**Jump cut.**

**LISTER**
What was that? Something weird just happened.

**KOCHANSKI**
Yeah, I felt it too.

**Jump cut.**

**CAT**
There it was again.

**Jump cut.**

**HOLLY**
And again.

**KRYTEN**
Oh my.

**LISTER**
What is it?

**KRYTEN**
I don't believe I'm here.

**KOCHANSKI**
I have that feeling all the time.

**KRYTEN**
I have it. I believe we're in some kind of computer-manipulated, psychotropically induced mind state.

**HOLLY**
You took the words right out of my mouth.

**KOCHANSKI**
You mean, this is our trial, our escape is our trial?

**LISTER**
The envelopes, when we signed the consent forms, there must have been some kind of drug on the gluey bit we licked.

**CAT**
So you mean nothing's been real since then? Blue Midget, the Ground Controller, none of that was real? You mean, after all this I still haven't got a date? Damn, another year when I have to send a Valentine card to my hand.

**LISTER**
But this is good, this is good. It proves we're innocent. Everything we've said and done - escaping, trying to track down the Nanos, it corroborates our story.

**HOLLY**
But you are guilty, guys. Who are you fooling? I don't know why I said that.

## 62 INT. AR SUITE - DAY

**Rimmer watches.**

## 62 INT. BLUE MIDGET - DAY

**KOCHANSKI**
We're being framed.

**Jump cut back.**

**KOCHANSKI**
Wait a minute, what's happening? I just said: 'We're being framed.' and suddenly -

**Another jump cut.**

**LISTER**
It just happened again. Everything we say is being ...

**Jump cut.**

**KRYTEN**
... bananas.

**LISTER**
If I say who I think's responsible for this it'll get cut too, so I'm not going to. But it's him, I know it's him, you can bet on it, and if I ever catch up with him I'm gonna cut off both his ...
(**Jump cut**) ... with a blunt knife.

**CAT**
So how do we stop it?

**KRYTEN**
If we're plugged into AR software there must be a trap door built into the program somewhere to allow escape.

**CAT**
You mean, to help you get out if the program freezes?

**KRYTEN**
Precisely. There'll be a cryptic clue around somewhere, something like a trap door or exit.

**They look around.**

**CAT**
I got it. There's a button here with E - Eleven - T on it.

**KRYTEN**
And?

**CAT**
Eleven is XI in roman numerals. E, X, I, T - exit.

**LISTER**
He got that?

**KRYTEN**
I think it proves without a shadow of a doubt this is not reality.

**KOCHANSKI**
Press it.

## 63 STOP FRAME ANIMATION SEQUENCE

**Plasticine world. They are all stop frame animation figurines.**

**Tight shot of the back of the cat's head.**

**Cat V/O:- Now where are we?**

**The Cat turns round and we see he is made of Plasticine.**

**KRYTEN**
Well, somehow we've wound up in the screen saver.

**KOCHANSKI**
We need to locate a power source so we can switch the AR machine off.

**LISTER**
Power source. Well, there has to be a clue around here somewhere. Maybe it's in this ice hole.

**Shark eats Lister and spits him out. Cat emerges from igloo.**

**CAT**
There's some food in here.

**KOCHANSKI**
So?

**CAT**
Including a bottle of ketchup.

**LISTER**
So?

**CAT**
Power ketchup. Get it?

**KRYTEN**
What's to get?

**CAT**
Power sauce.

**LISTER**
Pity he's only smart when he's made of Plasticine.

**KOCHANSKI**
Press it.

## 64 INT. MEDI-BAY - DAY

**The AR pods click open and they emerge as Rimmer furiously bangs the keyboard trying to work out what is wrong with the machine.**

**LISTER**
You back-stabbing, weaselly smegger. You were trying to frame us.

**RIMMER**
Listy, just the man, now I know at first glance this may look bad ...

**KOCHANSKI**
God, he's gorgeous.

**RIMMER**
Hold her back please, hold her. Please, no more. No more.

**KOCHANSKI**
Those nostrils - they're driving me crazy. I've simply got to have him.

**LISTER**
Hold her back, Krytie. Help me.

## 65 INT. SERVICE LIFT – EVENING. CONTINUOUS

**Rimmer backs in and frantically hits some lift buttons, trying to close the doors. The others enter too, restraining Kochanski.**

**Rimmer backs off doing his walk. The doors close.**

**KRYTEN**
Mr Cat, sir, put the lift on hold.

**Cat presses button.**

**KOCHANSKI**
I want his babies!!

**LISTER**
(To Rimmer) The Luck Virus, you still got it? Take some, it'll cure the virus and restore you both to normal.

**Rimmer takes tube out of pocket and swigs.**

**Kochanski goes back to normal and Rimmer loses his limp.**

**KOCHANSKI**
Oh, God, that's so embarrassing.

**Lister beams Holly onto monitor.**

**LISTER**
What now, Hol?

**HOLLY**
No time to lose, you should head for the nearest one of these ...

**Cam tilts so Holly's head looks like a moon.**

**LISTER**
You mean a moon?

**HOLLY**
Exactly.

**KRYTEN**
He's right. We can regroup there and continue our search for the Nanos.

**RIMMER**
What about me?

**KRYTEN**
Well, suggest we persuade you to come with us, sir, or failing that we bludgeon you unconscious.

**CAT**
Him? Come with us? Are you out of your mind? That's so dumb, I should have said it.

**KRYTEN**
Mr Rimmer has had access to the confidential files, sir, he knows all the security codes. Without him, our chances of escape are about as remote as meeting an interesting hairdresser called Kylie!

**RIMMER**
Why would I want to take off with you lot. What've you got to offer?

**KRYTEN**
Well, I'm very good at laundry, sir.

**HOLLY**
I do a damned fine moon impression.

**CAT**
I'm so gorgeous, there's a six-month waiting list for birds to suddenly appear every time I am near.

**KRYTEN**
And you know what they say, sir - if you've got three good friends you're a rich man.

**RIMMER**
Only poor people say that.

~~RIMMER~~
(To Lister) But what are you offering apart from the opportunity to watch you idle away your evenings tiddlywinking your verrucas into an old pair of boots?

**KOCHANSKI**
You used to do that?

**LISTER**
No, of course not. I always used to miss. Hardly ever got them actually in the boots.

**RIMMER**
I can't leave. I've got too much going for me here. What about my friends?

**LISTER**
What friends? You mean, the Polyester brothers - those saddos you play war-games with on Thursdays? When those guys get together they issue dandruff warnings on the news.

**KOCHANSKI**
Look, now you've been resurrected by the Nanos you've got a second chance, an opportunity to live your life afresh.

**KRYTEN**
~~And you know what they say, sir - if you've got three good friends you're a rich man.~~

**CAT**
Forget it. He's not going to change his mind. ~~We got more chance of persuading a dentist to hang around an X-ray machine.~~

**KRYTEN**
He's right, time is of the essence. The crew will know we're out of AR now and are probably sending someone to investigate.

**LISTER**
So, what's it to be?

**RIMMER**
Look, if I leave I'm always going to be a failure. The shame of it - everytime I have a boiled egg, knowing I don't even outrank the toastie soldiers. I want to be an officer, a man of honour ...

**LISTER**
Officers aren't men of honour. They're head cases. Those induction pranks they play when you qualify.

**RIMMER**
I've dreamt of that proud day for years now, as I wake up after the celebration party and find my pubes are orange and I'm handcuffed to a goat and, most hilarious of all, discovering someone's superglued me to the rear of one of those rabbits that whizzes round greyhound tracks. Aaah ... those mad japes they play on you - I can't miss all that.

**LISTER**
That's not going to happen for you now, man. Just like it didn't happen for the other Rimmer.

**HOLLY**
We're giving you a second chance at life and an opportunity for you to screw it up in a new and original way.

**KRYTEN**
You'll get your own seat in the cockpit, and you'll be in control of at least five buttons.

**KOCHANSKI**
Krytie, don't be pathetic, he's hardly going to be impressed at the prospect of being in charge of a few buttons.

**RIMMER**
(Impressed) Five, you say?

**LISTER**
No more vending machine maintenance. No more getting heckled by drinks' dispensers.

**RIMMER**
That's five whole buttons?

**KOCHANSKI**
A new start. A new life.

**LISTER**
You'll wake up in the morning and you'll want to leap out of bed.

**KRYTEN**
Well, in your case, Mr Lister, sir, that's because your sheets are covered in pointy poppadum shards.

**RIMMER**
Tell me more about these buttons. Are some illuminated?

**LISTER**
What do you say, man? The old Rimmer was a vital member of the team. He performed essential functions we've never replaced.

**RIMMER**
What did he do?

**LISTER**
Dunno really. He er ... he was em ... he was er ... **(Gets an idea)** ... Head of Safety.

**RIMMER**
Head of Safety, that's a hell of a title. What did he actually do?

**LISTER**
He sought out danger, he sought out peril and then he advised us the best way to run away from it.

**RIMMER**
Head of Safety. Five buttons. I'm in.

**CAT**
He's in. Let's celebrate. I'll crack open a bottle of cyanide.

## 66 INT. CARGO BAY - DAY

The posse creep across the cargo bay.

## 67 INT. BLUE MIDGET - DAY

As before they creep on board. Cat sits and starts up Blue Midget. A monitor buzzes into life, on it a face.

## 68 INT. GROUND CONTROL - DAY

A matronly type with glasses and a strange hat appears on screen.

**GROUND CONTROLLER 2**
This is Ground Control. You don't appear to have flight clearance.

## 69 INT. BLUE MIDGET - DAY

Cat reacts.

**CAT**
You're the Ground Controller?

## 70 INT. GROUND CONTROL - DAY

**GROUND CONTROLLER 2**
Please state your name and clearance code.

## 71 INT. BLUE MIDGET - DAY

Posse.

**CAT**
(To Lister) Reality sucks.

## 72 INT. GROUND CONTROL - DAY

**GROUND CONTROLLER 2**
Your name's Reality Sucks? **(Laughs)**
One second, Mr Sucks, just checking my clearance list.

## 73 INT. BLUE MIDGET - DAY

Posse.

**LISTER**
Look, just do another smegging dance and we'll get the hell out of here.

**CAT**
Dance? With her I'd have trouble walking. Powering up.

## 74 INT. LANDING STRIP - DAY
## CGI (MODEL)

**Blue Midget takes off and screams down the Landing Bay.**

**GROUND CONTROLLER 2**
Come back, Mr Sucks, come back.

## 75 CGI (MODEL)

**Blue Midget in space.**

## 76 INT. BLUE MIDGET - DAY

**Posse at stations.**

**KOCHANSKI**
There's nothing on the scanners for a thousand mile radius. We're in the clear, guys.

**ALL**
Yes.

**KRYTEN**
I don't believe we are, ma'am.

**CAT**
What's up?

**KRYTEN**
According to the supplies inventory we're frighteningly low - oh, and everyone was so happy. I can barely say it out loud.

**RIMMER**
What are we frighteningly low on? Oxygen?

**KRYTEN**
Worse, fabric softener. Suggest we chart a course to the nearest derelict, the SS *Einstein*, before everyone's woollens get all bibbly bobbly.

**CAT**
Einstein? Wasn't he the dude who discovered America.

**RIMMER**
Einstein discovered the Theory of Relativity.

**CAT**
Where did he discover it? Was it fossilised and stuff.

**RIMMER**
The Theory of Relativity is - what is the Theory of Relativity?

**LISTER**
Yeah, what is it, Hol?

**HOLLY**
Bit busy at the moment, Dave.

**LISTER**
Just tell us what it is. In sort of simple layman's terms.

**HOLLY**
It's a theory.

**LISTER**
Yeah, but what is it?

**HOLLY**
Oh, you want it more complicated than that, do you?

**LISTER**
What does it mean?

**HOLLY**
It's the Theory of Relativity. You know, it's the theory you only tell your relatives.

**KOCHANSKI**
E equals MC squared, what does that mean though?

**HOLLY**
E is energy. Energy equals MC squared. That's M times C timesed by another C.

**KOCHANSKI**
What is MC though?

**HOLLY**
What?

**LISTER**
What is it? MC?

**HOLLY**
MC - well, MC is obviously, uh, master of ceremonies.

**LISTER**
Energy equals Master of Ceremonies squared?

**HOLLY**
He was very over-rated, Einstein. That's why he left quantum physics and went into the look-a-like business.

**RIMMER**
It's so sad. Holly's supposed to have an IQ of 6,000, now I doubt he can even spell IQ.

**HOLLY**
If I'm so stupid, if I'm computer senile, explain this then.

**Pause.**

**CAT**
Explain what?

**HOLLY**
You can't, can you?

**LISTER**
Explain what?

**HOLLY**
It's no good stalling, trying to buy time. If I'm so stupid, explain why I was able to re-create a new set of Nanobots and get them to resurrect the crew?

**ALL**
What?

**HOLLY**
I thought you'd be pleased.

**CAT**
But why?

**HOLLY**
My job is to keep Dave sane, true I'm not that good at it - but I do my best. That's why I create these little diversions, to keep him occupied.

**LISTER**
But, Hol, we could have wound up doing two years in the brig.

**HOLLY**
You still could. I've just worked it out. We're still in AR.

**ALL**
What?

**HOLLY**
In computer jargon, my plans have all gone tits up. I was out thought and out manoeuvered.

## 77 INT. HOLLISTER'S OFFICE - DAY

We cut to the scene on a big screen and see Hollister and Holly, IQ 6,000, watching. Before them the guys including Rimmer are in AR.

## 78 INT. BLUE MIDGET - DAY

Posse.

**LISTER**
Who by?

**HOLLY**
By a superior intellect.

**CAT**
You mean the hand-drier in the men's toilets has out smarted you again?

**HOLLY**
No, by that other version of me. The one on Red Dwarf. This is still our trial.

**CAT**
Our trial? Why didn't you say? If I'd have known I'd have worn a tie.

## 79 INT. HOLLISTER'S OFFICE - DAY

Hollister and Holly (IQ - 6,000)

**HOLLISTER**
Well, for me, Lister's Nanobot story is corroborated, they were trying to track them down, their actions in the psychotropically induced scenario bear that out.

**HOLLY**
I agree, Frank. I also believe we died and were indeed resurrected. Again borne out by their actions.

**HOLLISTER**
So original charges - all innocent. But it's equally apparent that they used classified information from the crew's confidential files to their own ends. I suspected Rimmer had access the moment he walked into my office and began acting incredibly smart and knowledgable.

**HOLLY**
What a give away.

**HOLLISTER**
That's why I got him to lick one of the psychotropic envelopes when I invited him to dinner.

**HOLLY**
So abusing classified information, that's a fresh charge.

**HOLLISTER**
And on that they're all guilty.

**HOLLY**
That's a statutory sentence.

**HOLLISTER**
I know. Two years in the brig.

**HOLLY**
So instead of the original charge and a possible sentence of two years in the brig they've been found guilty on another charge and got an entirely different two years in the brig. That's going to be a great comfort to them. I'll bring them round and break the news.

80 INT. AR SUITE - DAY

**The posse in AR. They are released from AR.**

**RIMMER**
This is reality? But how can we be sure?

**CAT**
Why do we care? Nothing makes any sense, no matter where we are.

**LISTER**
Look, everything was real before we licked the envelopes, right? Then we conked out and got carted off to AR. Before we licked anything, before we licked anything, I lent you my Holly watch.

**RIMMER**
So if this is reality - I should still be wearing it.

**Rimmer looks - he's wearing the Holly watch.**

**HOLLY**
Oh yeah, this is reality all right. I'd recognise it anywhere.

**KRYTEN**
Also, sir, shouldn't you have the viruses? Again, you found them on Starbug before we licked the envelopes.

**Rimmer pulls viruses out of his pocket.**

**RIMMER**
The Luck Virus. Maybe we can get out of this mess?

**Hollister's hand comes into shot and confiscates it.**

**HOLLISTER**
I'll have that, the lab boys are gonna want to run tests on it. Where's the other one?

**Rimmer palms the Sexual Magnetism Virus to Lister.**

**RIMMER**
I'm afraid I lost it, sir.

**HOLLISTER**
Goddamn it, Rimmer - I wanted that. Uh, I mean, the lab boys wanted it - so they could test it too. Damn.

**KRYTEN**
(**To Rimmer**) This is all your fault.

**RIMMER**
My fault?!

**KOCHANSKI**
You betrayed us over that confidential files scam.

**LISTER**
Stole the Sexual Magnetism Virus.

**KRYTEN**
You lied to us.

**KOCHANSKI**
And generally behaved like a self-serving, scum-sucking, ruthless little ratbag.

**RIMMER**
And that's bad?

## 81 INT. MUG SHOT FLATAGE – *A LA* USUAL SUSPECTS

**HOLLISTER (Voice-over)**
It is the finding of this enquiry that you have been found guilty of contravening Act 21 of the Space Federation. Before sentencing you will have medicals so you can be assigned appropriate prison status.

**They stand in prison uniforms and have mug shots taken, including Holly.**

**HOLLY**
I've buggered this up a bit, haven't I?

## 82 INT. LIFT – DAY

**A finger presses a panel in the wall and the number '13' appears alongside the other numbers.**
**The finger presses it.**

## 83 CGI SEQUENCE

**Lift hammers down shaft.**

## 84 INT. FACTORY/PIPEY AREA – DAY

**They stand in line next to a bunch of the biggest, hairiest, shit-yourself-stupid, bad ass hombres. Ackerman stands above them.**

**ACKERMAN**
Welcome to the Tank.

**Lister takes the tube of 'Sexual Magnetism' and sprinkles it over Rimmer, who doesn't realise what he's done, and we see the terrified look on his face as all the hairies grin at him with a twinkle in their eyes and start touching him.**

## TITLES

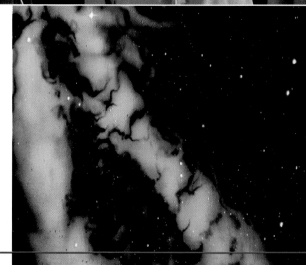

# BACKINTHERED
## PART THREE.

## *Cast & Crew*

Written by: **DOUG** NAYLOR

Rimmer: **CHRIS** BARRIE  Lister: **CRAIG** CHARLES  Cat: **DANNY** JOHN-JULES

Kryten: **ROBERT** LLEWELLYN  Kochanski: **CHLOË** ANNETT  Holly: **NORMAN** LOVETT

Hollister: **MAC** McDONALD  Ackerman: **GRAHAM** McTAVISH

First Ground Controller: **YASMIN** BANNERMAN

Second Ground Controller: **JEILLO** EDWARDS  MP Thornton: **KARL** GLENN STIMPSON


Casting Director: **LINDA** GLOVER  Choreographer: **CHARLES** AUGINS

Music: **HOWARD** GOODALL  **CLEMENT** ISHMAEL  Production Accountant: **MIKE** AMOS

Graphic Designer: **ANDY** SPENCE  General Manager GNP LTD: **HELEN** NORMAN

Location Manager: **KEN** HAWKINS  Production Co-ordinator: **RACHEL** STEWART

Post-Production Co-ordinator: **SIMON** BURCHELL

Stage Manager: **JACQUELINE** ZOPPI-TIGHE  Gaffer: **JOHN** BARKER

Props Master: **PAUL** DE CSERNATONY  Props Buyer: **TIM** YOUNGMAN

Art Director: **IAN** READE-HILL  Vision Mixer: **JOHN** BARCLAY

Engineering Manager: **ALAN** GODLEMAN  Camera Operator: **ANDY** MARTIN

Location Sound: **NIGEL** DAVIS  Sound Supervisor: **JEM** WHIPPEY  **Geoff** Moss

Editor: **MARK** WYBOURN  Script Associate: **PAUL** ALEXANDER

Script Supervisor: **GILLIAN** WOOD  First Assistant Director: **JULIE** SYKES

Visual Effects Designer: **JIM** FRANCIS  **Ed** Smith  **Mark** Howard

Digital Effects Designer: **CHRIS** VEALE  Make Up Designer: **ANDREA** FINCH

Costume Designer: **HOWARD** BURDEN  Line Producer: **JO** BENNETT

Production Designer: **MEL** BIBBY  Director of Photography: **PETER** MORGAN

Executive Producer: **DOUG** NAYLOR  Produced and Directed by: **ED** BYE

# INTRODUCTION
CASSANDRA.

The starting point for 'Cassandra' was the premise that the crew somehow come across a computer, which has the ability to predict the future with unerring accuracy. Similar to 'Future Echoes', in some respects, a crew member's death is predicted and they go to great lengths to avoid the inevitable but at each turn find they are getting nearer and nearer their predicted demise.

I decided this should happen to Rimmer because I felt the audience would believe we were going to kill him and resurrect him as a hologram.

I also had another idea, an idea for a movie, which I later find out is the same pitch as *Blake's 7* and *Armageddon*, which is: '*The Dirty Dozen* in space' - this was the Canaries.

I marry the two ideas to make 'Cassandra'.

In first draft form it's a two parter but on reflection I decide to cut half of the material and make it a one parter.

Ed and I get together with casting director, Linda Glover, and we start bandying around possible names to play the title role.

Linda suggests Geraldine McEwan, award winning actress (*Henry V*, *Oranges Are Not the Only Fruit*), whom she's convinced would be great in the part.

Ed and I laugh uproariously, believing we've got no chance of getting her.

Linda's not to be put off and says she's checked Geraldine's availability and, although she's free for our dates, at the moment she's shooting a movie in the States with Steven Spielberg's wife, Kate Capshaw.

Ed and I laugh even more uproariously and say let's see some other actresses for when Geraldine says 'no'.

Linda sends Geraldine the script.

Two days later we hear Geraldine loves the script and wants to do it.

Ed and I stop laughing and tell everyone who'll listen that Geraldine was our idea and we always thought she'd say 'yes'.

Geraldine comes to the read through and I know immediately she's going to be one of my all-time favourite guest stars along with Tim Spall in 'Back to Reality' and Jake Wood who was to play Kill Crazy, also in 'Cassandra'.

We film the show in front of the live audience, the audience is good but not as good as the utterly fantastic audience from the first recording - the original one hour special version of 'Back in the Red'.

I remind myself that a great audience reaction doesn't necessarily mean a great show. The audience for 'Back to Reality', the fans' favourite show, watched most of it in silence, only laughing when we recorded scenes for the second or third time.

'Cassandra' was my favourite show and I'm slightly disappointed with the reaction as we go back on location to shoot the inserts for the last four shows. I'm having breakfast at some ungodly hour before shooting begins and Robert Llewellyn wanders up wearing just his Kryten mask and a pair of football shorts, a sight I've never got completely used to, especially at six in the morning. Robert tells me his web page has been inundated with great feedback for 'Cassandra'. One of the emails says 'it's the best show we've ever done' and 'Red Dwarf will never die'.

Breakfast tasted good that day.

When the show is broadcast, Alan Rickman, who is a friend of Geraldine's - they worked together on *Robin Hood: Prince of Thieves*, watches the show, loves it and takes a copy to show Steven Spielberg, with whom he's about to work.

A few days later my Mum phones me, I recount the Spielberg story. She says: 'Hang on, let me get a pen, so I can write this down and tell your Father. Steven who?'

# RED DWARF VIII

## 'CASSANDRA'

### EPISODE 4

## Written by
## DOUG NAYLOR

# CASSANDRA

## TITLES

### 1 EXT. CGI SEQUENCE
Red Dwarf in space.

### 2 INT. CGI PRISON
Establisher of CGI prison.

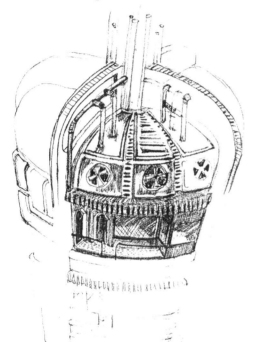

### 3 INT. PRISON QUARTERS – DAY
Lister enters. He accesses Holly.

**LISTER**
Have you figured a way to get us out of here yet, Hol?

**HOLLY**
I have actually, Dave. I've devoted all my run time to looking for a loop hole in the prison regs and I think I've come up with something which means you can serve your entire two year sentence in just 14 weeks.

**LISTER**
Ah, brilliant - what have I got to do?

**HOLLY**
Become a dog.

**LISTER**
A dog?

**HOLLY**
According to my data banks: dog years are 7 times shorter than human years. As a plan you can't fault it on its mathematics.

**LISTER**
No but maybe you can fault it on the fact that I'm not a dog.

**HOLLY**
Yeah, but according to a 20th-century newspaper called the *National Enquirer* the operation's quite straight forward: a roverostomy they call it. There's a photograph here of a bloke who had it done.

*NATIONAL ENQUIRER* - man becomes dog.
Photo of a dog.

**LISTER**
That's a dog.

**HOLLY**
You see how convincing it is, even you're fooled.

**LISTER**
Become a dog? That is without doubt the stupidest, crappiest, most pathetic plan you've come up with all week.

**HOLLY**
Give me a chance, it's only Monday.

~~**LISTER**~~
Anything else?

**HOLLY**
The only other way to get out is to convince them you're insane. Trouble is, according to prison regs: anyone who is insane wouldn't want to be released so anyone who claims they're insane to get out must be sane and therefore not eligible for release. It's a classic Catch 44 situation.

**LISTER**
Catch 22.

**HOLLY**
~~No, it's twice as bad as that.~~

He switches him off. Rimmer enters exhausted.

**RIMMER**
What happened to my life? Career, prospects, friends, I had everything and I threw it all away. It's a tragedy.

Z *Script cut from original broadcast.*

**LISTER**
What are you on about? You had none of that stuff.

**RIMMER**
You're right. I had none of that stuff, I had absolutely nothing and I threw it all away. It's an even bigger tragedy.

**LISTER**
We're only going to get through this by being positive. By being - what's that word women tennis players always used to reckon was so important ... begins with 'C'.

**RIMMER**
Cunnilingus?

**LISTER**
Centred, by being centred, focused. It's only two years. What with good behaviour it'll probably only be eighteen months. Remember when you were first born and then you were eighteen months - the time just flashed past.

**RIMMER**
It flashed past because you had two breasts, big as your head, at your beck and call, day and night. Give me that now and I wouldn't be wingeing. ~~How did I wind up in the brig with common criminals? Me? Someone with my upbringing and education. I bet I'm the only person here who knows how to spell 'symposium'.~~

**LISTER**
~~Yeah, but a skill like that's bound to come in dead handy in here. When the psycho-droids from G wing corner you in the laundry room you can say: 'Fellas, I think I should warn you, I know how to spell 'symposium'. They'll run a smegging mile.~~

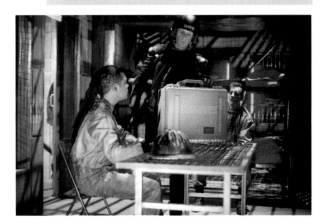

**Guard enters with package and hands it to Lister.**

**LISTER**
What's this?

**GUARD**
Canary outfits and first meeting information.

**Guard exits.**

**LISTER**
I've volunteered for the Canaries. Some bloke came round the machine shop so I signed up.

**RIMMER**
The Canaries?

**LISTER**
Yeah, you know, bit of close part harmony. You should see the list of privileges you get. Unbelievable.

**RIMMER**
You don't know what the Canaries are, do you?

**LISTER**
Of course I do. A singing troupe, *a cappella*. **(Sings in his most middle of the road voice)** 'You are the sunshine of my life, Oooo-ooo, that's why I'll always be a-round ...'

**Lister clocks Rimmer's smirk.**

**LISTER**
They're nothing to do with singing, are they?

**Rimmer shakes head.**

**LISTER**
Holly lied to me, didn't he? He was taking the smeg.

**RIMMER**
Oh, Listy - Listy, Listy, Listy.

**LISTER**
Well, go on then. What have I signed up for?

**RIMMER**
In the 19th century, when miners went down a pit, they'd lower a canary down first in a little cage.

**LISTER**
What and make them do some mining? They were sick in the 19th century, weren't they, eh? I mean, how much coal could a little canary get?

**RIMMER**

And if the atmosphere was noxious - as it frequently was - guess what the canary did?

**LISTER**

Complained to the foreman?

**RIMMER**

It died, Listy. The canary's job was to go into the most dangerous, unpleasant and smeggy situations and see if it could stay alive. Then they'd know if it was safe to send in the important people.

**LISTER**

I'm going to kill him.

**RIMMER**

How come you've never heard of the Canaries? They've got recruitment posters all over the men's bogs. How come you've not seen them?

**LISTER**

When I'm in the men's toilets in prison, Rimmer, I tend not to look around, you know what I'm saying? It's like playing golf, I concentrate on my grip, keep my eye on the ball and try not to veer off to the side.

**RIMMER**

The Canaries - you know what they say it's supposed to stand for? Convict Army Nearly All Retarded Inbred Evil Sheep-shaggers. (**Laughs**) They haven't got an 'X' chromosome to share between them.

**LISTER**

Smeg. It gets worse, as well.

**RIMMER**

(**Laughing**) Worse, go on.

**LISTER**

I've signed you up too. I forged your signature, I thought I was doing you a favour.

**RIMMER**

Me? Why?

**LISTER**

I signed us all up, Kryten, Kris, everyone.

**RIMMER**

No way, no way, no way am I becoming a Canary.

**4  INT.  FACTORY/PIPEY PARADE GROUND - DAY**

Line up of mean looking, mixed sex, marine types. Including our lot, and Blood Drinker.

**ACKERMAN**

It's a great honour for Floor 13, for today we are visited by Captain Hollister who has a special assignment.

**KILL CRAZY**

At last some action. I've been going mental, all this time cooped up, not killing nothing, yes!

**KNOT**

Kill Crazy, shut up, you punk.

**HOLLISTER**

OK, listen up. We've located a ship, the SSS *Silverberg*, buried at the bottom of an ocean moon. The remote probe's come back and with no signs of a crew, no bodily remains, no skeletons, zip. We want you guys to go on board and find out why.

Rimmer conducts and they begin *a cappella* version of 'You Are the Sunshine of My Life'.

**RIMMER**
One, two, a one, two, three, four ...

**DWARFERS**
(**Singing**) 'You are the sunshine of my life,
oooooooooooooo-oooooooooooooo,
That's why I'll always be a-ro-o-o-o-o-o-o-o-o-o-
o-o-o-ound ...'

**ACKERMAN**
Rimmer!

**RIMMER**
Sorry, sir, we appear to have wandered into the
wrong hobby group. We'll leave immediately.

**ACKERMAN**
You're here and this is where you'll stay. Now get
on with it.

**RIMMER**
Yes, sir. Thank you, sir. (**Addressing everyone**) You
heard what the Warden said, he wants us to get
on with it. From the top, 'You are the sunshine of
my life ...'

**ACKERMAN**
Rimmer!!

**RIMMER**
Sorry, sir. When you said: 'get on with it'...

**ACKERMAN**
Shut up. You're a Canary, man. A member of the
toughest convict army this side of Pluto. I've
seen custard factories that aren't as yellow as
you are. Start behaving like a man.

**RIMMER**
A man, sir. Yes, of course, sir, a man. A man.
Perhaps if you could just remind me, sir, I'm sure
it'd all come back.

**Rimmer gets beaten.**

**ACKERMAN**
Continue, Captain.

**HOLLISTER**
It's inconceivable a ship like this could be sent
out without a crew so whatever devoured the
crew, bones and all, might still be there. So, be
careful.

**KILL CRAZY**
Let's go kill something. Ye-aaah!!

## 5  MODEL SEQUENCE
**A crashed ship lies half buried at the bottom of the
ocean as a metal diving bell is lowered into the
murky depths from a chain.**

## 6  INT. DIVING BELL - DAY
**The Canaries plus Kill Crazy and Blood Drinker sit
like paratroopers preparing to be dropped in enemy
territory.**

**KILL CRAZY**
I hope it's got big teeth, and claws and like loads
of heads. Yeah! Great!!

**Posse react.**

## 7 MODEL SEQUENCE

**The diving bell lands on the side of the *Silverberg*,
like a limpet.**

**KRYTEN**
What? Where?

| PRODUCTION: RED DWARF VIII | PAGE: 1 |
|---|---|
| SHOW 2 : " CASSANDRA" | |
| SCENE: | P 14 |

*The diving
bell drops
into frame,
spotlights
blaze.*

*We tilt down
as it heads
towards the
murky,
crashed ship
below.*

*CUT TO:
The diving
bell
approaches
the side
of the Silver-
berg.*

*And attaches
itself onto an
airlock.*

## 8 INT DIVING BELL - DAY

**Kill Crazy unscrews airlock.**

**KILL CRAZY**
Here we go. At last. Yee-haaaaaaaa!!!

**He walks into the door frame and knocks himself
unconscious. The others walk past him into the *Silverberg*.**

## 9 INT. SSS *SILVERBERG* - DAY

**It's eerie. The Canaries pad down a corridor,
reach a crossroads and go off in various directions.**

**LISTER**
OK. Stay together, keep them peeled.

**RIMMER**
What's that?

**RIMMER**
It's moving, shaking from side to side, like a leaf.

**KRYTEN**
I think that's your shadow, sir.

**They walk on.**

**Kochanski appears out of a doorway.**

**KOCHANSKI**
Located the mainframe. Maybe it can tell us
something?

Yee-haaaaaaaa!!!

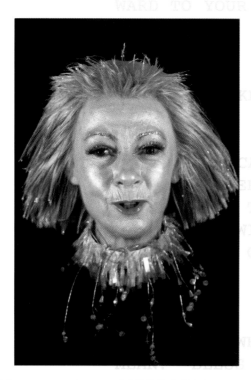

## 10 INT. CASSANDRA'S ROOM – DAY

A head, ephemeral and opaque, floats above a light source which projects it into the room.

**CASSANDRA**
Good evening, Arnold. I've been looking forward to your arrival so very much.

**RIMMER**
How do you know my name?

**CASSANDRA**
My name is Cassandra, I am a computer with the ability to predict the future with an accuracy rating of 100%. Bless you.

**RIMMER**
Bless you? What do you mean 'bless you'? ...
(Atchooo)

**CASSANDRA**
You need a tissue. Kris has one in her left hand pocket, she says: 'Would you like this?' You say: 'Thanks'.

Kochanski hands over tissue.

**KOCHANSKI**
Would you like this?

**RIMMER**
Thanks.

**CASSANDRA**
Extraordinary.

**KRYTEN**
Extraordinary.

**CASSANDRA**
The questions we can ask - it can tell us our future.

**KOCHANSKI**
The questions we can ask - it can tell us our future.

**CASSANDRA**
But how does it work? The future's not happened yet?

**LISTER**
I'm not going to say that.

**CASSANDRA**
I never said you would.

**LISTER**
But how does it work? The future's not happened yet?

**CASSANDRA**
Although you do.

**LISTER**
Smeg.

**RIMMER**
Let's ask her a question about the future. A biggie.

**LISTER**
OK, Cassandra - do we ever get back to Earth? Has the human race survived?

**CAT**
Do I ever find my singing tie-pin?

**KOCHANSKI**
Look, do we want to know all this stuff about the future? Do we want to know for example, how and when we die?

**RIMMER**
Kris's right, something like that could mess up your life forever. Cassandra, I have a question.

**CASSANDRA**
I know, Arnold, because I know the rest of this conversation.

**RIMMER**
So what's the answer?

**CASSANDRA**
He chokes to death, aged 181, trying to remove a bra with his teeth.

**LISTER**
What was the question?

**RIMMER**
I just asked how you died?

**LISTER**
You what? I didn't want to know that. Whose bra?

**CAT**
181 - probably your own.

**LISTER**
Come on though, taking a bra off with my teeth aged 181 - that's a hell of a sexy way to go.

**KRYTEN**
So long as the teeth are in your mouth at the time, sir.

**LISTER**
I'm really screwed up now. I didn't want to know that. Know how I die. It's completely spoilt the surprise.

**CASSANDRA**
Kryten, this is where you share your theory with your crewmates.

**KRYTEN**
I have a theory everyone. The *Silverberg* didn't crash, did it Cassandra? This ship was sent here by the Space Corps on auto-pilot to get rid of you. To abandon you at the bottom of a lunar sea in the depths of deep space.

**CAT**
That's brilliant, bud - how'd you work that out?

**KRYTEN**
I read it on this Mission Directive, here.

**Holds up paper.**

**LISTER**
So, there was no dead bodies on board because the ship didn't have a crew.

**KRYTEN**
A computer that unerringly predicts the future ...

**CASSANDRA**
... is a dangerous thing indeed.

**KRYTEN**
... is a dangerous, yes, precisely.

**Suddenly everyone is nervous.**

**RIMMER**
We, uh, should be making tracks.

**CASSANDRA**
I'm afraid that's not going to happen. The bulkhead's just given way and we're shipping water at 1,000 gallons a second. All the Canaries will be dead within one hour, except for Rimmer ...

**RIMMER**
Ye-es!!

**CASSANDRA**
... who will be dead in twenty minutes. Only Lister, Kryten, the Cat and Kochanski survive.

**LISTER**
What happens to Rimmer?

**CASSANDRA**
He has a heart attack brought on by the stress of knowing he's going to die and collapses, during a conversation with me, in nineteen minutes and thirty-one seconds.

**RIMMER**
I don't believe you, I simply don't believe you.

**CASSANDRA**
We shall see. Or rather you shall see. I have already seen.

**KOCHANSKI**
All the hairs on the back of my neck are standing on end.

**CAT**
Mine too and not just the ones on the back of my neck. It's one up all up.

## 11 INT. CARGO BAY TYPE AREA – DAY

**The gang sit around drinking coffee from flask.**

**LISTER**
(To Cat) Well, this isn't the first time we've been in a situation like this, is it?

**CAT**
Hell, no - we've drunk coffee thousands of times. We're veterans.

**LISTER**
Future Echoes, remember?

**CAT**
Future Echoes, oh right.

**KOCHANSKI**
What was that?

**LISTER**
Well, we learnt then, if the future's already decided you can't change it.

**RIMMER**
Yeah, but what do you know?
You're a chicken soup machine repairman not Hank Handsome, Space Adventurer. Don't get ideas above your station and your station is Git Central.

**LISTER**
Hey, I've been surviving in space for five, six years - when it comes to weirdy, paradoxy space stuff, I've bought the T-shirt.

**KRYTEN**
He bought it and I ironed it for him.

**LISTER**
Exactly.

**RIMMER**
So you're saying the future's the future and like your underpants the chances of change are remote? Well, I'm sorry, I don't accept it.

**LISTER**
Hey, I'm not happy about it, man.

**Cat touches Rimmer tenderly on the knee.**

**CAT**
None of us are. You dying is the last thing we want, bud. Especially me. Hell, I'll probably have to help dig the hole.

**RIMMER**
Right, so to summarise; six years of space adventuring, six years of experience and knowledge have led you to the conclusion that I'm totally stuffed.

**KRYTEN**
Mr Rimmer has a point, sir. Your greater knowledge is making you pessimistic while his ignorance and almost doe-like naivety is keeping his mind receptive to a possible solution.

**LISTER**
Shut your stupid flat head, you.

**KOCHANSKI**
(To Kryten) So you're saying: when you don't know enough to know that you don't know enough, there's no fear holding you back, you can achieve things which people with more brains can't.

**KRYTEN**
Precisely.

**KOCHANSKI**
He's got the power of ignorance.

**KRYTEN**
And with the ignorance he's got, that makes him one of the most powerful men that's ever lived. Harness your stupidity, sir. Employ your witlessness. Use your empty-headed, simplistic, moron mind and find a solution.

**RIMMER**
OK, I've got an idea. (To Kryten) Kryten - replay our meeting with Cassandra in your CPU and tell me if at any point anyone ever called me Rimmer.

**LISTER**
What?

**Kryten watches the scene in fast forward.**

**KRYTEN**
At no point throughout the meeting did anyone refer to you as Rimmer. In fact, we barely looked at you.

**RIMMER**
That's just what I thought. Cassandra said Rimmer dies but it doesn't necessarily follow that that means me.

**LISTER**
Who does it mean then - your Dad?

**RIMMER**
Look, Cassandra doesn't know the future, she sees pictures of it, she could have seen some other guy die of a heart attack, someone she's been told is called Rimmer.

**KOCHANSKI**
He's right.

**RIMMER**
All I've got to do is find someone I can introduce to Cassandra as Rimmer, and it will be them that stiffs out and not me.

**KRYTEN**
Such low-life conniving, it's impossible not to be impressed. What I wouldn't give to have your weasel gene, sir.

**Kryten suddenly realises Rimmer is staring at Cat.**

~~**KRYTEN**~~
Permission to leave the room before you utter your next sentence, sir.

**RIMMER**
Permission refused.

**KRYTEN**
No, not me, sir.

**RIMMER**
But you're perfect. A mechanoid. Disposable.

**KRYTEN**
But what about our relationship, sir? After everything we've been through, surely you have feelings of warmth and affection for me?

**RIMMER**
I've only known you a week. I don't give a stuff.

**KRYTEN**
Of course. He hardly knows me.

**CAT**
Me and you both.

**KOCHANSKI**
Hang on. During the Cassandra meeting, you referred to Kryten as Kryten several times.

**KRYTEN**
Therefore Cassandra knows I'm Kryten and consequently I can't be Rimmer. ~~You'll need to find some other poor sap to set up.~~

**Rimmer's eyes light up as he looks at the Cat.**

**CAT**
Now, wait a minute.

**KRYTEN**
Oh, look, here's Mr Knot.

**Knot enters. Rimmer's face lights up with delight.**

**KNOT**
You've made this area secure?

**RIMMER**
Yes, sir, Mr Knot, sir. Coffee, sir?

**Knot nods.**

**KNOT**
I've been asked by the Captain to inspect the mainframe. Where is it?

**Rimmer hands him a cup and pours it over him by mistake.**

**KNOT**
You idiot - what the hell do you think you're doing?

**RIMMER**
Please, have my jacket. I insist.

**They swap jackets. Rimmer brushes the name tag with his name on it as Knot puts it on.**
**We didn't see this under his space suit in previous Cass scene.**

**RIMMER**
Then I shall lead you to Cassandra. There we are, sir, a perfect fit, sir.

**KNOT**
Lead the way, Rimmer.

**RIMMER**
Don't call me Rimmer.

**KNOT**
That's your name.

**RIMMER**
Yes, but 'Rimmer', it's so full of nobility and quiet courage. Call me Arse Wipe or Fish Breath but not Rimmer, sir, never Rimmer, sir.

**KNOT**
OK, Arse Wipe, whatever you say. Now where's the mainframe?

## 12 INT. CASSANDRA'S ROOM – DAY

**Rimmer and Knot enter.**

**CASSANDRA**
Hello, Arnold, bang on time.

**RIMMER**
I've brought you a visitor, Cassandra. Do you know his name?

**CASSANDRA**
Yes, I do. Not ...

**RIMMER**
(Clutching chest) What?

**CASSANDRA**
Not ...

**RIMMER**
Knot?

**CASSANDRA**
Let me finish, not that it matters, what his name is, I mean, our relationship doesn't last very long.

**Rimmer whimpers with relief.**

**KNOT**
I understand you have the ability to predict ...

**CASSANDRA**
... the future, yes I do.

**KNOT**
100% reli-

**CASSANDRA**
-able. Yes.

**KNOT**
What happens to me? Do I get back to earth?

**CASSANDRA**
No, you die in about four seconds time. Of a heart attack after hearing the news that you're going to die of a heart attack.

**KNOT**
You filthy lia-

**Knot has heart attack.**

**CASSANDRA**
Poor Rimmer.

**RIMMER**
Yes, poor old Rimmer.

**Knot collapses.**

**KNOT**
My name is Knot ...

**RIMMER**
Your name is not what?

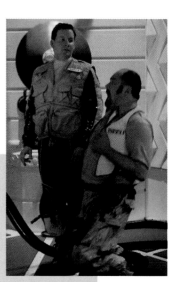

**KNOT**
Knot, ~~Knot ... Knot, Knot~~..

**RIMMER**
(Still trying to cover) Who's there?

**KNOT**
(Dying) Yurggghhhhh.

**RIMMER**
~~Yurggghhhhh who?~~

**Knot dies.**

**RIMMER**
Is he dead now?

**CASSANDRA**
I'm afraid so.

**RIMMER**
Ye-es!!

**CASSANDRA**
He died of a massive coronary. Just as I prophesied.

**RIMMER**
Ye-es.

**CASSANDRA**
You seem inordinately happy, Arnold. But why? You're going to die too.

**RIMMER**
But you said I ... I'm going to die too?

**CASSANDRA**
I already told you, Rimmer dies of a heart attack and then you and all the other Canaries die too. All except Lister, Kryten, Kochanski and the Cat. I've seen it.

**RIMMER**
That's as well as maybe but have you seen this?

**Rimmer gives her the finger.**

**CASSANDRA**
Yes, I'm afraid I have.

## 13 INT. CORRIDOR - DAY

**RIMMER**
You were right, there's nothing I can do.

**KRYTEN**
According to Cassandra, our future is decided and we four survive. Therefore, while we are here, we cannot die. Regard.

**Kryten takes out a gun and shoots himself through the head. Gun jams. Points it at others, gun jams again. Points at Rimmer.**

**KRYTEN**
Duck, sir.

**Rimmer ducks, bullet blasts into wall.**

**KRYTEN**
Duck again, sir. As I thought.

**CAT**
So in other words if I ...

**Cat hits Lister on shoulder with fire axe.**

**LISTER**
Aggghhh. What's that for?

**CAT**
You can't die.

**LISTER**
Yeah, but I can feel pain, you smegger.

**KRYTEN**
So, how about this: we use our powers of invulnerability, which will last until we return to Red Dwarf and surround Mr Rimmer, escort him up to the Obs Deck and into the diving bell.

## 14 INT. CORRIDOR - DAY

**Lift doors open. Rimmer in the middle, them holding onto him, surrounding him, shuffle down the corridor.**

~~**RIMMER**~~
Bravo, Krytie. I've got to take the ~~old boater~~ off to you on this one. (**To ~~Koch)~~ Kr**is, could you press a bit harder. ~~Don't be afraid to really squash your~~ bosom into me. After all this is ~~my life we're protecting. 100% effort.~~

**Finally.**

**LISTER**
The diving bell. We've made it.

**The group part but Rimmer is no longer in the middle. They look around baffled.**

**KOCHANSKI**
Where'd he go?

**They walk back the way they came. There is a hole in the walkway. Rimmer on the floor groaning.**

**LISTER**
Yo!

## 15 INT. DECK BELOW - DAY

**Kochanski is lowered into shot on a rope. She lands.**

## 16 INT. CORRIDOR - DAY

**CAT**
Hear that?

**KRYTEN**
Water.

**LISTER**
(Calls) Kris, take cover the water's coming.

**CAT**
Quick the diving bell.

## 17 INT. DECK BELOW - DAY

**Kochanski and Rimmer run along. Jump through an airlock and seal the door. We hear the water rush past.**

## 18 INT. DECK BELOW THE DECK BELOW - DAY

**KOCHANSKI**
Great, everything above us is flooded, and now we're back down in the

bowels again with Cassandra.

**RIMMER**
It's coming true, my death, it's all coming true.

## 19 INT. CASSANDRA'S ROOM - DAY

**Rimmer enters disconsolate.**

**CASSANDRA**
You tried to cheat the future and failed as I knew you would.

**RIMMER**
So what happens now? How, how do I die?

**CASSANDRA**
Lister catches you making love to Kochanski, and shoots you through the head with a harpoon gun.

**RIMMER**
Can you just double check that?

**CASSANDRA**
I have seen it. It's what happens. In the old laundry room.

**RIMMER**
So let me just repeat what I think you're saying. Arnold, that's me and Kochanski, that's the woman, the really attractive one you saw earlier, me and her, we're in bed, giving it riz, when Lister, that's the short dumpy one with the stupid haircut, walks in and shoots me through the head while I'm making love with Kochanski?

**CASSANDRA**
That is what is going to happen.

**RIMMER**
Fantastic.

## 20 INT. LAUNDRY ROOM - DAY

**Rimmer is making the bed.**

**KOCHANSKI**
I can't believe what you're telling me.

**RIMMER**
I can scarcely believe it myself. I mean, obviously you're incredibly attractive, I never thought you'd look at me twice.

**KOCHANSKI**
Neither did I.

**RIMMER**
But apparently we're going to make love. Unbesmegginglievable, or what? It's not warm in here - fancy a wee nip?

**KOCHANSKI**
Oh, no, no, no.

**Rimmer pours some whisky.**

**KOCHANSKI**
But why would I want to sleep with you? I mean, it doesn't make sense.

**RIMMER**
Maybe you get blind drunk?

**KOCHANSKI**
That doesn't excuse my other four senses.

**Rimmer turns on tap to fill it with water.**

**RIMMER**
Right, barely an hour to go. Shall we get started? I mean, let's face it: you can't change the future. **(Beat)** Sadly.

**KOCHANSKI**
But you said you could.

**RIMMER**
Yeah, I've changed my mind now.

**Turns on second tap, still no water.**

**KOCHANSKI**
Look, you sure you wouldn't prefer to play the Opera Game instead?

**RIMMER**
Kris, it's what Cassandra saw. You can't cheat fate.

**KOCHANSKI**
Well, just watch me, because there is no way on earth I'm climbing out of my clothes and clambering into that bed.

**Rimmer turns on third tap. She gets soaked with water.**

**KOCHANSKI**
My clothes are soaking.

**RIMMER**
Why don't you take them off, and dry them on the heater.

**KOCHANSKI**
**(Horrified)** It's coming true, it's all coming true.

**She starts to drink the whisky.**

**RIMMER**
**(Delighted)** It's coming true, it's all coming true.

## 21 MODEL SEQUENCE - DAY.

**Diving bell is in the sea being pulled up to the surface.**

## 22 INT. DIVING BELL - DAY

**Lister is suited up. Cat and Kryten stand by. Kill Crazy still unconscious, moaning slightly.**

**CAT**
Bud, you can't go back there.

97

**LISTER**
Cassandra said Kris survives. The only way that's going to happen is if someone goes back in and saves her. Chuck us that harpoon gun, will you?

## 23 INT. LAUNDRY ROOM - DAY

**Time cut: Kochanski is in a makeshift bed of sheets and blankets, Rimmer sings some mood music and joins her on the bed.**

**KOCHANSKI**
I'm not sure about this, this is the first time I've ever been seduced by pre-determinism theory.

**Rimmer climbs into bed with her, wearing T-shirt.**

**RIMMER**
One hour exactly.

**The door opens and the light goes on and Lister walks in, holding harpoon.**

**RIMMER**
Oh, bloody, buggering hell. Tonight must be the night they put the clocks forward.

**LISTER**
I've got it.

**RIMMER**
That's more than I did.

**LISTER**
I've worked it all out.

**RIMMER**
I never get any breaks, ever. (**To Kochanski**) Twenty seconds later and you could have been on top and I could have used you as a human shield.

**KOCHANSKI**

I must have been mad. What the hell was I thinking. I felt sorry for you.

**LISTER**
Look, will you shut up and listen to me.

**KOCHANSKI**
Why aren't you mad that I'm in bed with him?

**LISTER**
Because I know why you're in bed with him and I also know that I don't kill him.

**KOCHANSKI**
Oh, but Cassandra promised.

**LISTER**
Cassandra made that up to force you two together, so that you'd feel sorry for him and hopefully end up sleeping with him.

**RIMMER**
So why did she say she saw it happen?

**LISTER**
To try and make it happen.

**KOCHANSKI**
But why?

**LISTER**
To try and punish me.

**RIMMER**
Punish you? Why?

**LISTER**
Because Cassandra knows, and has always known, how she dies. And she was trying to make me suffer now for something that I'm destined to do in the future.

**RIMMER**
You kill her? Don't you? That's why she hates you, because she knows you're going to kill her.

**LISTER**
That's what this whole thing was about. Kryten figured it out.

**RIMMER**
Kryten figured it out, did he? Good old Kryten. But did he really have to figure it out quite so damn fast? Would it have killed him to take 30 minutes longer. Ten minutes even. Two would have done ...

**LISTER**
I'm gonna take care of the rest of it now. I'll see you two love birds later.

**Lister exits.**

**RIMMER**
Look, thanks for being with me tonight, I can't think of anyone I'd rather share my final hour with than you and I really mean that. I'm not all bad, in fact sometimes I'm quite sweet and sensitive.

**KOCHANSKI**
(Moved) Bye.

**RIMMER**
By the way -

**Rimmer holds up her knickers.**

**RIMMER**
Is it OK if I keep these?

## 24 INT. CASSANDRA'S ROOM – DAY

**Lister stands before Cassandra.**

**LISTER**
If the future's all worked out, horoscopes, all that stuff, it means we're not responsible for anything we do. It means we're just actors saying lines, in a script that's been written by somebody else. I don't want to believe that. I want to believe I'm in charge of my own life, my own destiny, so I'm not going to kill you, Cassandra. I'm out of here.

**CASSANDRA**
But you do kill me, I've seen it.

**LISTER**
Tomorrow's a new day, a fresh page in a book that's not been written yet. What happens in the future is up to me, not some pre-determined destiny smeg. I'll see ya, kidder.

**Lister walks out in triumph, sticking some gum on the wall as he exits, which drops off, causing a chain reaction, which results in whisky tipping into Cassandra's works which causes her to blow up.**

**LISTER**
Smeg.

## TITLES

# CASSANDRA

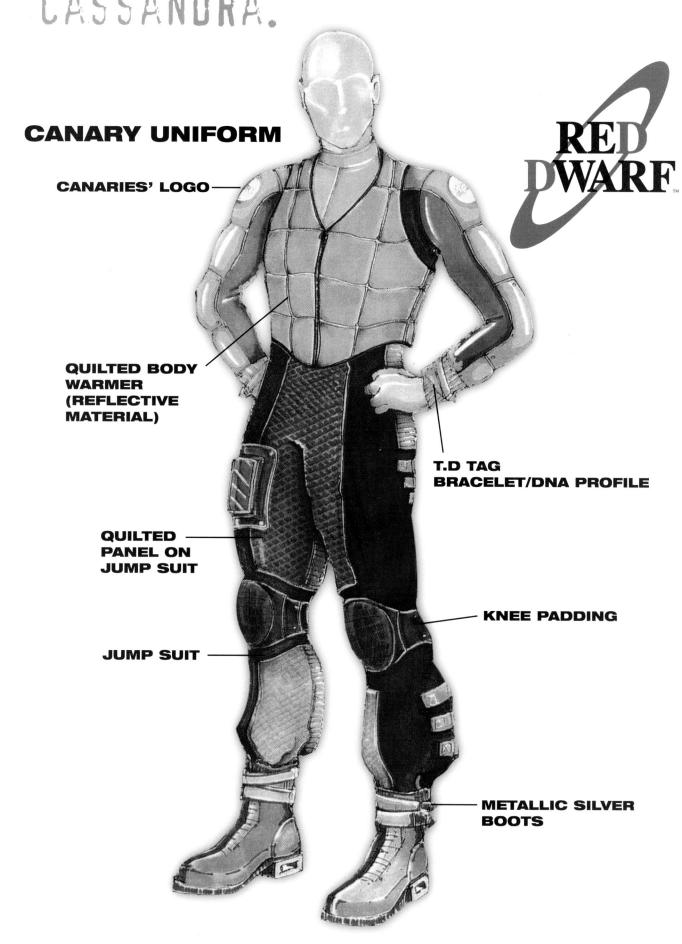

## CANARY UNIFORM

**CANARIES' LOGO**

**QUILTED BODY WARMER (REFLECTIVE MATERIAL)**

**QUILTED PANEL ON JUMP SUIT**

**JUMP SUIT**

**T.D TAG BRACELET/DNA PROFILE**

**KNEE PADDING**

**METALLIC SILVER BOOTS**

RED DWARF™

# OUTRO CASSANDRA.

Craig Charles has got a Rolls Royce.

It's a 1977 Silver Shadow. The kind of car you expect Tom O'Connor or Jim Bowen to drive.

It's Craig's pride and joy.

He won't let anyone smoke in it, apart from him and his kids, and no-one and I mean no-one, is allowed to eat fish and chips in the back.

He loves it that much.

I'm surprised he's not put a sign up in the back: 'Kindly refrain from eating fish and chips while travelling in this motor vehicle. Thanks, in advance, The Owner. P.S. No kebabs either.'

He used to park his Roller under his first storey dressing room window, in a car parking space next to mine, and gaze at it adoringly in breaks from rehearsal.

No-one ever took the piss out of him for this.

Except for Robert. And Danny. And Ed. And me. And Chloë. And Norm.

Chris didn't. Chris was probably staring at it adoringly too.

One day, I was over in our offices at the David Lean building at Shepperton Studios looking at some video covers. I don't know who used to be responsible for making the covers - we use Andy Spence now - but they never, *never* let us see them until they've managed to spell at least half the cast's names wrong. 'Red Dwarf, starring Chris Barry and Charles Craig, Robetrt Lewelyn, Danni Jon-Jewels, Norman Lovit and Chloe Anet.'

I've spent at least two years of my life in video cover meetings.

The video cover people then usually like to take a photograph that's out of focus, ideally from the wrong series, carefully ensuring the member of the cast is in the wrong costume before they get a colour-blind ape to draw a starfield with his left foot. Then they invite me to a meeting and ask me what I think of the cover.

Then when I say I don't like it they assume that very calm air people assume when working with people who are 'difficult perfectionists'.

I was attending one of these meetings during the shooting of 'Cassandra', and trying to persuade them that using the word 'zany' more than seven times on the same video cover wasn't good, when my mobile rang.

It was Ed, he said they were about to start shooting and to get over there pronto.

I ran to my car, started it, made the one minute journey to the sound stage and screeched to a halt in my car parking space outside the studio.

Well, that was the idea.

In my haste I pranged the car in the parking space next to mine.

It was Craig's Rolls Royce.

Somehow, I'd managed to get my front bumper bar snagged over his rear bumper. It looked like the two cars were mating.

I had to reverse off it.

As I did, there was a terrible clanging noise.

I couldn't bear to look at his car, so I looked at mine first.

My bumper had been ripped off and was lying on the floor.

Unknown to me, VT editor, Mark Wybourn, stood watching.

He did what any normal guy in his position would have done. Roared with laughter and went off to tell everyone.

I looked at Craig's Roller.

There wasn't a mark on it. Not a single scratch.

It was still in mint condition.

What do they build those cars out of?

Mine was in bits.

People started hanging out of windows, watching me survey the wreckage.

Suddenly, two of Jim Francis's special effects guys appeared, jacked my car up, replaced the bumper, rewired the electrics and everything was as good as new in less than ten minutes.

I couldn't decide whether to tell Craig; after all, his car was undamaged and it wasn't a story he was going to enjoy.

At the end of series party, I finally plucked up courage and told him.

He took it really well.

He didn't hit me.

Not even once.

# CASSANDRA

CASSANDRA.

## *Cast & Crew*

Written by: **DOUG** NAYLOR

Rimmer: **CHRIS** BARRIE  Lister: **CRAIG** CHARLES  Cat: **DANNY** JOHN-JULES

Kryten: **ROBERT** LLEWELLYN  Kochanski: **CHLOË** ANNETT  Holly: **NORMAN** LOVETT

Special Guest Star As Cassandra: **GERALDINE** McEWAN  Hollister: **MAC** McDONALD

Ackerman: **GRAHAM** McTAVISH  Kill Crazy: **JAKE** WOOD  Warden Knot: **SHEND**

Guard: **IAN** SOUNDY  Blood Drinker: **JOSEPH** CRILLY


Stunt Co-ordinator: **NICK** GILLARD  Casting Director: **LINDA** GLOVER

Music: **HOWARD** GOODALL  Production Accountant: **MIKE** AMOS

Graphic Designer: **ANDY** SPENCE  General Manager GNP LTD: **HELEN** NORMAN

Location Manager: **KEN** HAWKINS  Production Co-ordinator: **RACHEL** STEWART

Post-Production Co-ordinator: **SIMON** BURCHELL

Stage Manager: **JACQUELINE** ZOPPI-TIGHE  Gaffer: **JOHN** BARKER

Props Master: **PAUL** DE CSERNATONY  Props Buyer: **TIM** YOUNGMAN

Art Director: **IAN** READE-HILL  Vision Mixer: **JOHN** BARCLAY

Engineering Manager: **ALAN** GODLEMAN  Camera Operator: **ANDY** MARTIN

Location Sound: **NIGEL** DAVIS  Sound Supervisor: **JEM** WHIPPEY  **Geoff** Moss

Editor: **MARK** WYBOURN  **Dave** White  Script Associate: **PAUL** ALEXANDER

Script Supervisor: **GILLIAN** WOOD  First Assistant Director: **JULIE** SYKES

Visual Effects Designer: **JIM** FRANCIS  **Ed** Smith  **Mark** Howard

Digital Effects Designer: **CHRIS** VEALE  Make Up Designer: **ANDREA** FINCH  Costume Designer: **HOWARD** BURDEN  Line Producer: **JO** BENNETT

Production Designer: **MEL** BIBBY  Director of Photography: **PETER** MORGAN  Executive Producer: **DOUG** NAYLOR  Produced and Directed by: **ED** BYE

# INTRODUCTION
KRYTIE TV.

Most of the crew and cast's favourite episode was 'Krytie TV'. Not maybe the most spectacular in terms of SFX but most of them believed it to be the funniest. Which in a way is weird because no script in Red Dwarf history has undergone as many rewrites.

As a rule of thumb the best shows are the easiest to write, usually going though only four or five drafts. Up to Series VIII 'Tikka to Ride' had probably the most drafts with about twelve, 'Back in the Red 1 and 2' had fifteen before I even handed them in, but 'Krytie TV' was somewhere in the twenties and was regarded for the first seventeen or so of those rewrites to be an absolute dog.

It started with a script conference with Paul Alexander, Ed and I.

I wanted to know what was happening to Kryten in the women's wing. We talked about the possibility of Kryten having showers with the girls, that someone would persuade him to film, and then him getting the idea to develop his own TV station. Paul wrote the first two drafts, I wrote a third and then the bloodshed began.

Ed liked the idea and thought the shower night stuff was funny but the script then fell away badly.

After about twelve drafts I showed it to my wife and asked her what she thought.

'Be brutally frank,' I said.

'OK,' she said. 'It's stupid, immature, and mostly unfunny.' Rimmer, she correctly observed, was hardly in it. 'It's all about Kryten,' she went on, 'and the most successful shows have Lister/Rimmer spines but this show has nothing for them to do.'

I took this in good spirit and within a week I'm talking to her again.

Back to the drawing board.

I holed myself up in a hotel and started frantically thinking of Lister/Rimmer spines. At the time I'd been working on a show about Lister's guitar, inspired by something Craig had told me. I'd asked him if you were allowed to have a guitar in prison. He said 'yes' but they'd probably remove the strings to stop you garrotting fellow inmates. I'd written a couple of scenes on this subject but the script 'No Strings Attached' wasn't going anywhere. I read through my notes, there was an idea about Lister sabotaging Kochanski's ex-boyfriend's quarters, leaving prawns on the hot table lights and sprinkling his pubes over the bed sheets. I threw out eighty per cent of the original script and started again.

Six drafts later, I handed the script in.

The read through went well and then I took it away to tweak it.

More drafts.

Finally we get to the recording night and Robert can't remember any of the lines in his scene with Craig on the balcony, when he asks him if he's heard the bad news. There's so much repetition in the scene it's really tough to remember.

Craig suggests they ad lib it. They know the skeleton of the scene it doesn't matter if the odd word changes.

I can't believe I'm agreeing to this. I've written twenty drafts of this bloody script and I'm agreeing to Craig and Robert improvising the opening of the scene.

It's time for the recording, they improvise the 'bad news section'. Craig and Robert are brilliant.

I wonder if I can get them to do whole shows like this? 'Guys, I've got this idea where you come across this deserted space-craft and something funny happens. OK, go out there and improvise.'

# RED DWARF VIII

## 'KRYTIE TV'

### EPISODE 5

## Written by
## DOUG NAYLOR

## &

## PAUL ALEXANDER

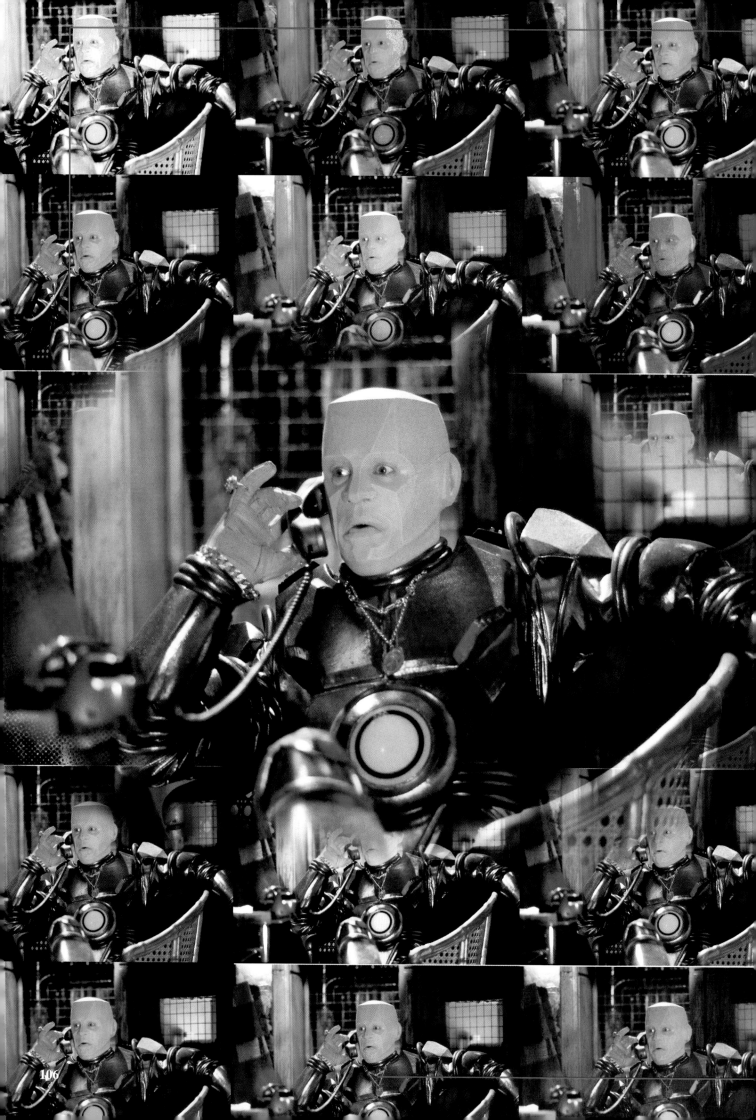

# KRYTIETV

KRYTIE TV.

## TITLES

### 1 CGI/MODEL SEQUENCE

Red Dwarf in space.

Music:- 'Sometimes It's Hard to Be a Woman'

### 2 INT. ENTRANCE TO WOMEN'S WING - DAY

Sign: 'Women's Wing'. Kryten enters with Kochanski.

### 3 INT. EXERCISE AREA - DAY

The women prisoners - including Kochanski and Kryten - are all skipping.

### 4 INT. PRISON CELL - DAY

Kochanski is painting her nails red. We see Kryten also has a bottle of nail varnish and he has painted his entire foot.

### 5 INT. PRISON SHOWERS - DAY

Steamy. Women in towels stand in line waiting for showers. Kryten stands behind Kochanski reading and holding a folded umbrella. Towels drop to the floor and the women step into the showers. Kryten puts his umbrella up and walks into the shower too. Still reading he walks along under the line of shower heads.

Z   *Script cut from original broadcast.*

## 6 MODEL SHOT

**CGI Prison establisher.**

## 7 INT. PRISON QUARTERS – DAY

**Rimmer lies on bunk. Lister pokes his head round door.**

**LISTER**
The post's arrived.

**RIMMER**
Brilliant, a bit of excitement at last.

**Lister walks in carrying a small wooden post.**

**LISTER**
Look at that, it's a beaut. (**Off Rimmer's look**) One of the struts has collapsed on my bed. I think it was those beans.

**Lister chucks letters on table and starts fixing his bunk.**

**LISTER**
Oh, the mail. Haven't had a chance to look. Anything from my mates?

**Rimmer sieves through mail.**

**RIMMER**
Don't think so. There's nothing here in orange crayon with half the letters backwards.

**LISTER**
Anything for you?

**RIMMER**
Just the usual, a couple of death threats and I'm in the *Reader's Digest* lucky dip. Apparently, I'm one of the special few selected for their lucky dip.

**LISTER**
That'll be you and the other twelve zillion people then, will it?

**RIMMER**
I've won either a holiday in Mauritius, a soft-top sports car or a fabulous matching set of egg cups. 'Scrape with a coin to discover which'. (**Scrapes**) I've won the holiday.

**LISTER**
What?

**RIMMER**
Three million years into deep space where I can't claim it and I go and win a smegging holiday in Mauritius.

**Opens second letter.**

**RIMMER**
They're taking the smeg.

**LISTER**
What now?

**RIMMER**
I've won the lottery as well.
To collect your cheque simply
bring your winning ticket to Lottery House, 24 Argyle Street. Four million. No luck, that's my problem. No luck at all.

**LISTER**
It's just a wind-up from the guards to sap our morale.

**Opens third letter.**

**RIMMER**
Here's one for you.

**LISTER**
Who from?

**RIMMER**
Petersen. (**Reads**) My God. That is tragic!

**LISTER**
What's happened to him? Has he died?

**RIMMER**
Died? You think he'd write and tell you?

**LISTER**
You're right, you're right. I'm not thinking straight, he'd be too busy with his funeral and everything, wouldn't he? What's happened to him?

**RIMMER**
Something catastrophic. Hideous. He's found your guitar in Starbug's wreckage and he's sending it here.

**LISTER**
Brilliant!! Are you OK?

**RIMMER**
Of course, I'm not OK. I hate your guitar. If I wanted to share a cell with an irritating lump of wood, I'd have moved in with an Australian soap star.

**LISTER**
Have you got a problem with me and my guitar, Rimmer?

**RIMMER**
It's not just me, even your goldfish wince and they haven't even got ears.

**LISTER**
I didn't realize you thought I was that bad.

**RIMMER**
Didn't you get a clue that time I tried to insert it in you.

**LISTER**
You would have stood a better chance if you'd used the neck end. Anyway you were revising, you always get a bit uptight when you're revising. Come on, come on, what about the 'Om song' that was a classic. (**Sings**) Oommmmmm-mm!

**RIMMER**
People who heard that formed self-help groups.

**LISTER**
Don't give me that. They played my demo on hospital radio.

**RIMMER**
Yes and three patients came out of comas, packed their bags and went home.

**Guard enters with guitar, hands it to Lister, face down. Guard exits.**

**LISTER**
Hey, hey, the axe man is back, you beaut. (**Turns it over**) Hang on, there's no strings. They've confiscated the strings.

**RIMMER**
I feel like a man who leaps out of a plane with no parachute and lands in the hot tub at the *Playboy* mansion.

**LISTER**
Why would they take my strings? It doesn't make sense.

**RIMMER**
Prison regs, you're not allowed anything you can hang yourself with.

**LISTER**
But I wouldn't want to hang myself if I had my guitar strings.

**RIMMER**
I think they were thinking of me. Maybe my luck's changing. At last a break.

**Guard re-enters.**

**GUARD**

Oh, by the way, you've both been commissioned to clean out the sewers. It's either that or go on a suicide mission.

**RIMMER**

See what I mean? Lucky, lucky, lucky. Suicide mission, please.

**LISTER**

Make that two suicides.

**GUARD**
Oh, by the way, I forgot, for you.

He hands Lister a letter. Lister opens it and reads.

**LISTER**
Because of the nature of your crime blah blah blah we are willing to review your case. For this process to be successful you would need a record of good behaviour and accept the consequences that a successful appeal would mean similar amnesty for prisoner colleagues in your situation.

**LISTER/RIMMER**
Yes!!

8 MODEL SEQUENCE

The Canary drop ship in space.

Caption:- 2 days later.

9 INT. CANARY DROP SHIP - DAY

We track down a line of Canaries. 4 or 5 attractive women, including Kochanski, chat away.

**KOCHANSKI**
Well, thanks to Kill Crazy, that was the least enjoyable suicide mission I've ever been on.

**KILL CRAZY**
And I was standing there, right? And right in front of me was this weird sort of mutant thing, with like two heads and all these tentacles - it took one look at me, and ran off. Why d'you think it done that? (Checks his breath)

We arrive at Kryten talking to the guys.

**KRYTEN**
(Whispered) ... You don't know what it's like being classified as a woman, sir, the humiliation.

**LISTER**
(Not listening) Yeah, I know, I know.

**KRYTEN**
I mean why should I, a series 4,000 mechanoid, have to endure the turgid monotony of showering with the girls - 3 times a week? Tell me that?

**LISTER**
(Bored) It's not fair, I know. It's just that - you shower with the girls?

**KRYTEN**
It's so hideously dull, I can't describe it. They stand around soaping themselves, their bodies all wet and foamy.

All the Canaries are listening now.

**KRYTEN**
Can you imagine it?

He stops - suddenly aware that all the guys are all staring into the mid-distance.

**KRYTEN**
Oh, my goodness, we've just been frozen in time again. Hello?

He waves his hand in front of them.

**KRYTEN**
Extraordinary. It must be a warp in the time/space continuum - how curious it isn't affecting me.

**RIMMER**
We're not frozen in time, Krytie. We were just thinking about what you were saying.

They all cross their legs in unison.

**HOLLY**
It's times like this that make me thankful I'm just a head.

**KILL CRAZY**
Oi, Droid-Boy! Oi! Next time you're in the showers, why don't you ... you know, smuggle in a camera and film 'em. Eh? Yeah, that'd be brilliant! Oi, I haven't seen a naked woman since ... well, ever. Yeah, I'd pay you. What'd you say?

**RIMMER**
No! I forbid it.

**LISTER**
Yeah, me t- **(Realizes what Rimmer's just said)** ... what?

**RIMMER**
It's voyeuristic, exploitative, and immature ...

**HOLLY**
All right. Who are you and what have you done with our Rimmer?

~~**CAT**~~
Let me get this straight - a hidden camera filming the girls' shower night, and you're voting 'no' to the 'Soapy Bosom' Party.

**RIMMER**
Dreadful idea.

**CAT**
I did just mention these girls would be naked and soapy, not forgetting soapy, but especially remembering naked.

**RIMMER**
I understand the concept.

**CAT**
Do you understand the meaning of the words: 'naked' and 'soapy' though? This is crucial to my ~~point.~~

**RIMMER**
Gentlemen, allow me to clarify my position. Morally speaking, using a hidden camera in the women's showers and taking shots of them, sudding themselves with mounds of foam, without their permission, morally speaking, I'm speaking morally here - I'm all in favour. However, Listy's been invited to appeal and a scam like this could ruin it.

**CAT**
Appeal?

**LISTER**
Yeah. I'm appealing.

**HOLLY**
That's a minority view.

**RIMMER**
Look, if he's successful, we can all be successful. We've just got to be model prisoners.

**KILL CRAZY**
Screw his appeal. I wanna see skin.

**CAT**
Yeah. Whaddya say, bird tray head?

**KRYTEN**
Are you asking me to betray the people I live with? To ignore their humanity and reduce them to mindless sex objects merely there for your moronic titillation?

**CAT**
Yes, please.

**KRYTEN**
If you'll excuse me, I forgot who I was for a moment.

**KILL CRAZY**
What are you doing?

**KRYTEN**
I'm a woman and proud of it. If you'll excuse me, I'll be with my fellow sisters - doing it for ourselves.

**Kryten goes over and sits with the women.**

## 10 MODEL SEQUENCE
**Red Dwarf.**

## 11 INT. PARADE GROUND - DAY
**The prisoners stand on parade.**
**Ackerman enters, wearing dark glasses and carrying a bucket.**

**ACKERMAN**
I'm going to make this quick and easy. Last night, on D-Wing - I was beaten up and mugged.

~~**CAT**~~
**(Whispered)** That's good of him to tell us, I needed a lift.

**ACKERMAN**
When I came round, I discovered something of great sentimental value had been taken from me.

**RIMMER**
(Whispered) Probably his gonad electrocution kit.

~~**Ackerman is handed a bucket.**~~

**ACKERMAN**
You have one chance. I'm going to turn the lights off for precisely 10 seconds - during which I want whoever took it ...

**He takes off his shades, he's wearing an eye patch.**

**ACKERMAN**
... to return my glass eye!

Ackerman puts a bucket down.

**ACKERMAN**
Kill the lights.

Darkness.

**ACKERMAN**
10, 9, 8, 7, 6, ...

Something clangs into the bucket.

The lights come on again. He reaches into
the bucket.

**ACKERMAN**
I'm glad to see good sense prevailed.

He pulls out a pair of dentures.

**ACKERMAN**
I have a date with Miss Patricia
Carling from Supplies on Saturday night. She thinks my eyes are
my loveliest feature!!
If I go like this I'm only HALF
LOVELY! ~~I want my eye back!~~ (**Calm**) If it's not
returned in the next 30 seconds, all Canary
privileges suspended - one month.

**RIMMER**
I know who stole your left peeper, sir.

Rimmer points to huge man standing next to him.

**RIMMER**
It was him, sir. I saw him playing marbles with it
this morning, sir.

Huge man swings at Rimmer, Rimmer ducks.

Guards arrest huge man and find the eye.

**ACKERMAN**
Thank you, Rimmer.

They start to file out.

**KOCHANSKI**
Have you gone mad? You don't rat on other inmates. It's an unwritten law.

**RIMMER**
Look, if it helps the appeal, what else matters? Model prisoners.

**CAT**
You're dog meat, bud. From now on everyone's going to be after you.

**RIMMER**
What for ratting on Saddo? Nonsense. He had no mates. He was a loner, friendless and pathetic.

Rimmer is suddenly attacked by a load of prisoners.

**KRYTEN**
But that wasn't Saddo, sir. That was Chummy, his much loved twin brother.

Rimmer continues to get beaten up.

**RIMMER**
It's so hard telling them apart.

## 12 INT. PRISON CORRIDOR - DAY

The Canaries are returning to their quarters. Lister and Rimmer walk along together with Cat and Kryten bringing up the rear.

A piece of screwed up paper rolls out in front of Kryten. Unable to pass it by, Kryten picks it up, takes it over to a nearby waste disposal on the wall.

**KRYTEN**
Would the sky really fall in if people just tidied up a little?

A service hatch next to the disposal opens and a hand clutching a wrench smashes Kryten on the head - and drags him back through hatch. Cat continues walking oblivious.

An unconscious Kryten is injected with something, we just see their hands. (It's Kill Crazy)

## 13 MINIATURE SEQUENCE

Black and white. A flying saucer in space, shot like a 1950s, S/F movie.

The saucer lands unsteadily on earth.

## 14 INT. STREET - DAY

A group of people watch, open mouthed, including some children.

All the men and male children are dressed identically, suits and glasses, women also identical 50s stuff.

## 15 MINIATURE SEQUENCE
The door of the saucer opens shakily.

## 15 INT. STREET - DAY

A man runs down the street.

**MAN IN FILM**
They're here, they've landed.

**WOMAN IN FILM**
Who have?

**MAN IN FILM**
The aliens, the invisible aliens.

The man points at nothing in particular.

**MAN IN FILM**
Look there's one!

**WOMAN IN FILM**
And there's another!

Everyone screams and runs.

## 16 INT. PRISON CINEMA/MESS HALL - DAY

Lister, Rimmer and Cat, mouths open, watch transfixed.

**VOICE-OVER**
From the people who brought you *Vampire Bikini Girls Suck Paris*, comes another cinematic masterpiece - *Attack of the Giant Savage Completely Invisible Aliens.*

Superimposed on screen:
*Attack of the Giant Savage Completely Invisible Aliens.*

**VOICE-OVER**
Marvel at the special effects, marvel at the high fidelity sound ...

**LISTER**
Looks like another pearler.

**CAT**
Why do they always show us these lousy B movies?

**RIMMER**
To sap our morale. Next week it's the George Formby season. Get your hanging rope now while there's still some left.

Suddenly the screen blips out and Kryten stands talking to camera. He is holding a hand mirror and transmitting this image via his optical receptors.

**KRYTEN**
Good evening. Tonight's scheduled feature has been cancelled and replaced by a special, live, pay-per-view event brought to you courtesy of Krytie TV. Transmitting live by my optical receptors, we bring you live and lithe: *Women's Shower Night.*

Sporty title music as Kryten whips the mirror away and we see the P.O.V. shot of where he is standing - in front of a door marked 'Women's Showers'.

## 17 INT. PRISON CINEMA/MESS HALL - DAY

Much cheering amongst the audience.

**CAT**
They really going to show this? No way! This is a joke right? This is - OH MOMMA!!

**LISTER**
You know what this means, don't you?

**CAT**
There is a God?

**LISTER**
They got to him. They reprogrammed Kryten.

Lister glares over to Kill Crazy, who sits grinning. We hear showering women noises.

**RIMMER**
(Transfixed) If we get caught watching this, your appeal's dead in the water.

**LISTER**
Forget the appeal ...

**CAT**
I already have.

**LISTER**
... what about Kris, she's never gonna believe I wasn't involved in this? We've got to stop it.

**RIMMER**
You're right. I want no part of this.

**LISTER**
Me neither.

**RIMMER**
We've got to go.

**LISTER**
Right now.

**RIMMER**
Not a minute to lose.

**LISTER**
I'm dust.

**RIMMER**
Me too.

**RIMMER**
After two. One, two, go!

**(Beat) Neither of them budge.**

~~LISTER~~
You're still here.

**RIMMER**
I could have sworn I left. I remember now, I came back to get you. Let's go.

**LISTER**
You got it.

**Neither moves a muscle. Eyes straight ahead.**
~~(A beat)~~

## 18 INT. SHOWER ROOM - DAY

**KRYTEN**
And now - I'm going to stare at a cracked floor tile.

## 19 INT. PRISON CINEMA/MESS HALL - DAY

**KILL CRAZY**
What's he doing that for?

**Large prisoners in 'Krytie-TV' T-shirts move amongst the audience with buckets.**

## 20 INT. SHOWER ROOM - DAY

**KRYTEN**
Remember, *Shower Night* is a pay-per-view event. Start filling those buckets.

## 21 INT PRISON CINEMA/MESS HALL

**Inmates make donations.**

**RIMMER**
I can't believe this, he's running it like a business, there's even a bloke over there selling ice creams.

**LISTER**
Never mind him, now, we've got to go.
Right now.

**RIMMER**
I'm going, I'm going.

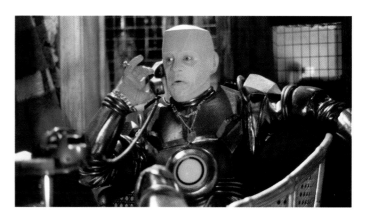

## 22 INT. SHOWER ROOM - DAY

**KRYTEN**
But now let's get up close and personal with one of the showerees. Miss Kristine Kochanski.

## 23 INT PRISON CINEMA/MESS HALL

**They both stop.**

**RIMMER**
Fancy a choc ice?

**They sit.**

## 24 INT. KRYTEN'S NEW UPMARKET PRISON QUARTERS - DAY

**Next day. The cell's an Aladdin's cave of hooky goods. Kryten is on the telephone.**

**KRYTEN**
OK, splendid, later.

**A guard escorts Lister to cell.**

**GUARD**
Mr Kryten, a visitor, sir.

**Kryten tips the guard. He exits.**

**LISTER**
Kryten - Look I know Kill Crazy's reprogrammed you, turned you into a ruthless entrepreneur, but I think I know how to change you back.

**KRYTEN**
Well, keep it to yourself, sir? I'll make it worth your while.

**LISTER**
Can't you see what it's done to you?

**KRYTEN**
It's made me rich, feared and respected. I'm loving every minute of it. I just bought the rights to the five-a-side soccer tournament today. Tomorrow I'm hoping to get the boxing.

**Kochanski enters.**

**KRYTEN**
Ah! Miss Kochanski - good to have you back. I have a little gift for you.

**KOCHANSKI**
Oooh, another one?

**KRYTEN**
Nothing's too good for you, ma'am. You know you were worried about picking up verrucas in the shower room, well, I've got the perfect solution - a water-proof pogo stick.

**Lister to one side.**

**LISTER**
(Whispered) This has got to stop.

**KRYTEN**
(Whispered) But that pogo stick could put the ratings through the roof, sir. Think of the money. Think of the show.

**LISTER**
(Whispered) I'm crazy about her. I'm not going to let you do this.

**KOCHANSKI**
Do what?

**LISTER**
(To Kris) How d'you think Kryten got all this?

**Lister hands her a piece of paper.**

**KOCHANSKI**
(She reads) *Shower Night Live*. Oh God is he paying some of the girls to do this? (Laughs)

**LISTER**
Who's that with the sponge?

**KOCHANSKI**
(Squints) That's me!

**LISTER**
It replaced the Wednesday night movie. I saw the whole thing. All three terrible hours of it. It was awful.

**KRYTEN**
Is that the time? I've got a merchandising meeting in two minutes. Excuse me ...

**Kryten exits.**

**KOCHANSKI**
You are dead, nickel-hydride breath. I'm having you melted down, made into a 1000 Tamagotchis - then I'm gonna starve them to death one by one! (To Lister) ... And you!

**LISTER**
What have I done?

**KOCHANSKI**
You were there for three hours of it?

**LISTER**
Yeah, but I didn't enjoy it. I was outraged - why do you think I only had one choc ice?

**KOCHANSKI**
How could you go along with this?

**LISTER**
I'm only human. You were completely naked, starkers, nude, in the buff, totally kitless, no clothes on.

**KOCHANSKI**
You've seen me with no clothes on. When we went out.

**LISTER**
Yeah, but I wanted to see if anything had changed.

**KOCHANSKI**
But why didn't you just ask? Instead of filming me in secret.

**LISTER**
Cos you'd have said 'no'.

**KOCHANSKI**
Not necessarily. If I'd known it meant that much to you - that you needed to see me naked so badly - I wouldn't necessarily have said no.

**LISTER**
You wouldn't?

**KOCHANSKI**
No, we're friends, aren't we?

**LISTER**
It never occurred to me that I could just ask. Oh, you're such a great friend. I love being your friend. (**Pause**) Kris?

**KOCHANSKI**
No! Not now! And now, not ever!

She shreds leaflet and chucks the paper-confetti at him.

**LISTER**
But you just said ...

**KOCHANSKI**
We're not friends any more.

She leaves.

## 25 CGI PRISON
Prison establisher

## 26 INT. PRISON CELL - DAY
Lister is sitting at the table with two small bags of flour, writing in a little card. Rimmer enters with a massive batch of appeal papers.

**RIMMER**
Appeal applications, Listy. Character testimonials. What's this?

**LISTER**
Kris found out about the shower thing. She went ballistic. It's a little present to say 'sorry'.

**RIMMER**
A bag of flour?

**LISTER**
No, two bags. (**Off Rimmer's look**) I'm in the Tank in the middle of deep space. I can't just get on the blower to Interflora you know, flour - flours, it's the closest I could get.

**RIMMER**
You romantic fool.

**LISTER**
You know how hard it is getting this stuff. I had to nick this from the bakery. She'll appreciate that.

**RIMMER**
I can just see her reading the card. 'Dear Kris, I'm really sorry for ogling you and the girls in the shower yesterday for three gob-smacking hours of steamy fun. To make up for it, and to indicate how truly sorry I am, here's two bags of self-raising. Something I didn't need any help with yesterday.'

**LISTER**
It's easy for you. You're not crazy about her. It's really debilitating being nuts about someone. You lose twenty IQ points every time you talk to them.

**RIMMER**
You must be nuts about a fair few people then, are you?

Kryten walks in with bags.

**KRYTEN**
The girls found out about *Shower Night*, they attacked me, cleaned out my system and kicked me out. I've been reclassified as a man.

## 27 INT. BALCONY - DAY

**Time cut. Lister and Kryten stand.**

**KRYTEN**
I feel terrible, sir, for endangering your appeal.

**LISTER**
It's not your fault, Kryten. They got to you.

**KRYTEN**
I presume you've heard the news about Ms Kochanski.

**LISTER**
What news?

**KRYTEN**
You haven't heard?

**LISTER**
Heard what?

**KRYTEN**
The news.

**LISTER**
What news?

**KRYTEN**
You haven't heard the news?

**LISTER**
Heard what news?

**KRYTEN**
No-one's told you?

**LISTER**
Told me what?

**KRYTEN**
About Ms Kochanski.

**LISTER**
What about Ms Kochanski?

**KRYTEN**
About Ms Kochanski and her ex-boyfriend, Tim?

**LISTER**
What about Ms Kochanski and her ex-boyfriend, Tim?

**KRYTEN**
I can't believe you don't know.

**LISTER**
Know what?

**KRYTEN**
No-one told you?

**LISTER**
Told me what?

**KRYTEN**
You mean to say, you're standing there blissfully unaware of the news about Ms Kochanski and her ex-boyfriend, Tim?

**LISTER**
What news about Ms Kochanski and her ex-boyfriend, Tim?

**KRYTEN**
I don't believe it!

**LISTER**
Believe what?

**KRYTEN**
I'm so traumatized. No-one's had the guts to tell you the horrible, terrible, terrible, appallingly hideous, awful news. I'm not sure I can even speak now.

**LISTER**
Kryten, there's a two-hundred-foot drop down there. Now tell me the news.

**KRYTEN**
Well, she's started going out with Tim again. He's taking her to the Officers' Club tonight. Probation permits it provided she's back by 10.

**LISTER**
Oh, this is all down to that shower thing, isn't it?

**KRYTEN**
You know what Tim's like, sir? Impossibly handsome, oozes charm, a great lover. And you're just you. It's so unfair. You must feel awful.

**LISTER**
Well, I do now. God.

**KRYTEN**
You're taking this very well, sir. I'm really impressed.

**LISTER**
No, I'm not, man. I'm falling apart.

**KRYTEN**
I know that, but I was just trying to cheer you up.

**They exit.**

## 28 INT. PRISON QUARTERS – DAY

**Lister and Kryten enter. Holly on screen.**

**LISTER**
What can I do?

**HOLLY**
You've got to deal with your grief, man.
A break-up is very much like a bereavement.
It's usually followed by a cremation and some sandwiches.

**LISTER**
You haven't got a clue what you're on about, have you?

**HOLLY**
Mark my words. Time is a great healer, unless you've got a rash in which case you're better off with ointment.

**LISTER**
Look, they haven't seen each other for ages. They're only going out for a meal. What's the worst thing that can happen?

**RIMMER**
How's this, Listy? A little wine, a little laughter, then it's back to his place for coffee and a game of chess, before you know it she's sandwiched between two Bishops and her Queen's exposed to an attack from the rear.

**KRYTEN**
It's a tragedy.

**LISTER**
What are you so bothered about? I thought you hated the idea of me and her getting it together.

**KRYTEN**
Oh, that's the old me, sir. I've grown and matured since then. No, the new me wants you to have children so I can iron those itty bitty little socks and you're not getting any younger sir. And neither are your sperms. I'm getting worried about those guys. Any older and they'll need a Stannah stair lift to get up the Fallopian tubes.

**LISTER**
So what do you propose?

**KRYTEN**
We nail that horny stag and get you and the divine Ms K together. It's my way of saying 'sorry'.

**RIMMER**
But nothing that's going to endanger the appeal.

**KRYTEN**
First - we sabotage the date.

**LISTER**
What, we?  You mean you're going to help me?

**KRYTEN**
Step on board the Love Express, sir.

**Kryten unrolls a map onto the table.**

**KRYTEN**
Now, you get to his quarters through the air-vents. I've paid off the guards. Then you make him look like the nerdiest slob in the entire universe! Now this is what you leave in his quarters.

**Kryten opens the bag.**

**KRYTEN**
A half-eaten onion sandwich. That's always a passion killer.

**LISTER**
Is it? I like those.

**KRYTEN**
And then there's this. *Morris Dancer Monthly*. What a total dweebo, nerdmeister he'll look with those.

**RIMMER**
They're mine.

**KRYTEN**
And then there's these. Tragically unfashionable underpants.

**RIMMER**
They're mine.

**KRYTEN**
And finally Christian rock music ... If that doesn't scare her off - nothing will.

**RIMMER**
Have you been going through my things?

**KRYTEN**
And not forgetting ...

Kryten holds up some scissors.

**LISTER**
A pair of scissors?

**KRYTEN**
This is the *pièce de résistance*.

## 29 INT. TIM'S QUARTERS – DAY

An air-vent falls into the room. Lister sticks his head out, panting and sweating.

Time cut.

Lister races around leaving the magazine and the underpants and onion sandwich etc.
He leaves the music.

**LISTER**
Frank Assisi and the Apostles - *Hymns in Rock*. Digestive biscuit.

He sprinkles some biscuit crumbs on bed. Finally he takes out the scissors and unzips his flies. There is a snipping noise and he comes up with a handful of hair. He throws back the duvet and sprinkles his pubes liberally over the bed sheet, then races across and leaves a clump sticking out of the soap.

**LISTER**
The love assassin.

Lister fires his finger and blows it like a smoking gun.

## 30 INT. MESS HALL – DAY

The prisoners watch Lister on a giant screen, laughing, including a perplexed Rimmer.

On the giant screen Kryten stands in -

## 31 INT. CORRIDOR OUTSIDE TIM'S QUARTERS - DAY

- wearing a Jeremy Beadle type beard pretending to wash the floor.

**KRYTEN**
... what Mr Lister doesn't know, of course, is he's been set up by Krytie TV. Sssh, here he comes now.

The door opens, Lister makes sure the coast is clear and then emerges.

**KRYTEN**
Mr Lister?

**LISTER**
Kryten, is that you?

**KRYTEN**
You trashed that room because you believed Ms Kochanski was dating Tim, didn't you?

**LISTER**
What, do you mean she isn't?

**KRYTEN**
Look whose quarters you've really trashed.

Lister looks at the name plate on the door. It reads: 'Mr Ackerman'.

**LISTER**
But you said the girls had restored you back to normal.

## 32 INT. MESS HALL - DAY

On screen the scene is played out.

## 33 INT. CORRIDOR OUTSIDE TIM'S QUARTERS - DAY

**KRYTEN**
Ooops, you've been Krytered!!

The prisoners laugh and applaud.

**LISTER**
I've wrecked Ackerman's quarters?

## 34 INT. MESS HALL - DAY

**RIMMER**
The appeal!!

Rimmer exits.

## 35 INT. CORRIDOR OUTSIDE TIM'S/ACKERMAN'S QUARTERS - DAY

Lister tries the door which is locked.

**KRYTEN**
And the surprises haven't finished yet, here on Krytie TV, because Mr Ackerman and his red-hot date are due back any second. Sir, it's a race against time. Start cleaning that room.

Rimmer appears out of a grille.

**RIMMER**
Sorry to keep droning on about this but what about ... (Screams) the appeal!!

**LISTER**
Smeg!

Rimmer and Lister leg it down the corridor, and climb into an air duct.

## 36 INT. ACKERMAN'S QUARTERS - DAY

Lister and Rimmer dive out of the air duct.

**RIMMER**
Ah, smeg!

They start madly tidying the quarters. They go to leave.

**LISTER**
Statue?

**Rimmer picks up statue.**

**Lister remembers soap.**

**LISTER**
Aaaaaaaaaahhhhhh!

**Lister runs over to the sink and removes the pubes from the soap and hands it to Rimmer to carry.**

## 37 INT. CORRIDOR - DAY

**They fall out of Ackerman's exhausted.**

## 38 INT. MESS HALL - DAY

**Prisoners applaud and throw money in buckets. As on screen we see.**

## 40 INT. CORRIDOR - DAY

**KRYTEN**
Thanks for watching, folks. See you next time.

**RIMMER**
There he is.

**LISTER**
Kryten, come here a minute.

**They start chasing Kryten down the corridor.**

**KRYTEN**
I was just trying to boost the ratings, sir.

**LISTER**
Get him. Then back to the Tank.

**KRYTEN**
It was nothing personal.

**Kryten starts to leg it with some P.O.V. work.**

## 41 EXT. CGI SHOT

**Prison establisher.**

## 42 INT. PRISON QUARTERS - DAY

**Rimmer sits. Lister enters, waving a brown letter.**

**LISTER**
The appeal.

**Lister opens and reads.**

**LISTER**
(**Punching air**) Yes!!

**RIMMER**
(**Reads**) 'Dear Mr Lister, your appeal has been successful. From this day forth all inmates with no records of violence or depression will be allowed to have strings on their guitars.' This appeal was all about guitar strings?

**Lister takes a packet of strings out of the envelope.**

**LISTER**
You didn't think it was about getting out of here, did you?

**RIMMER**
You mean to say I've been busting my balls so you can have strings on your lousy stinking guitar?

**LISTER**
You've been a brick, man. And as a personal thank you, I thought I'd write you a song.

**Rimmer sits, looking horrified.**

# TITLES

# KRYTIE TV

## Cast & Crew

Written by: **DOUG** NAYLOR & **PAUL** ALEXANDER

Rimmer: **CHRIS** BARRIE   Lister: **CRAIG** CHARLES   Cat: **DANNY** JOHN-JULES

Kryten: **ROBERT** LLEWELLYN   Kochanski: **CHLOË** ANNETT   Holly: **NORMAN** LOVETT

Kill Crazy: **JAKE** WOOD   Ackerman: **GRAHAM** McTAVISH   Man in Film: **MARK** CAVEN

Woman in Film: **SARAH** WATERIDGE   Guard: **CLIFFORD** BARRY


Casting Director: **LINDA** GLOVER   Music: **HOWARD** GOODALL

Production Accountant: **MIKE** AMOS   Graphic Designer: **ANDY** SPENCE

General Manager GNP LTD: **HELEN** NORMAN   Location Manager: **KEN** HAWKINS

Production Co-ordinator: **RACHEL** STEWART

Post-Production Co-ordinator: **SIMON** BURCHELL

Stage Manager: **JACQUELINE** ZOPPI-TIGHE   Gaffer: **JOHN** BARKER

Props Master: **PAUL** DE CSERNATONY   Props Buyer: **TIM** YOUNGMAN

Art Director: **IAN** READE-HILL   Vision Mixer: **JOHN** BARCLAY

Engineering Manager: **ALAN** GODLEMAN   Camera Operator: **ANDY** MARTIN

Location Sound: **NIGEL** DAVIS   Sound Supervisor: **JEM** WHIPPEY   **Geoff** Moss

Editor: **MARK** WYBOURN   Script Supervisor: **GILLIAN** WOOD

First Assistant Director: **JULIE** SYKES   Visual Effects Designer: **JIM** FRANCIS

**Ed** Smith   **Mark** Howard   Digital Effects Designer: **CHRIS** VEALE

Make Up Designer: **ANDREA** FINCH   Costume Designer: **HOWARD** BURDEN

Line Producer: **JO** BENNETT   Production Designer: **MEL** BIBBY

Director of Photography: **PETER** MORGAN   Executive Producer: **DOUG** NAYLOR

Produced and Directed by: **ED** BYE

# INTRODUCTION
## PETE - PART ONE.

A meeting. Me, Ed and Chris Veale sit around throwing ideas about.
'How much are dinosaurs?' I ask.
'Dinosaurs?' said Ed suddenly alarmed.
'Yeah, how much do they cost? I keep hearing these stories about how cheap CGI is now. I was just wondering how much they actually cost. I realise we'd probably need two, one CGI and one animatronic. But how much would a CGI one cost?'
Chris Veale knew the answer. 'There's a Spanish one I might be able to get on the cheap.'
'A Spanish one?'
'The Spanish do a very reasonable dinosaur. It's a CGI wire-frame, and costs about one hundred and fifty quid.'
'A hundred and fifty quid, you can't be serious?'
'It's true.'
'Even we can afford a hundred and fifty quid.'
'That's obviously just for the wire-frame. Once you've got that then obviously I'd have to add skin texture and animate it. But if you've got the wire-frame it saves all that time actually designing it.'
'Do they do cats? I had this idea that the miniaturised Starbug could come across Frankenstein in the air ducts and fly up its bum and the Cat would be saying something about this being the Holy Mother and Lister would do a Tarantino-type line about it being the holiest of holies.'
'No, they don't do cats.'
'Pity.'
'They do rats though.'
'Rats?' I say. Mmm - interesting.

29.10.98

# RED DWARF VIII

## 'PETE - PART 1'

### EPISODE 6

## Written by
## DOUG NAYLOR

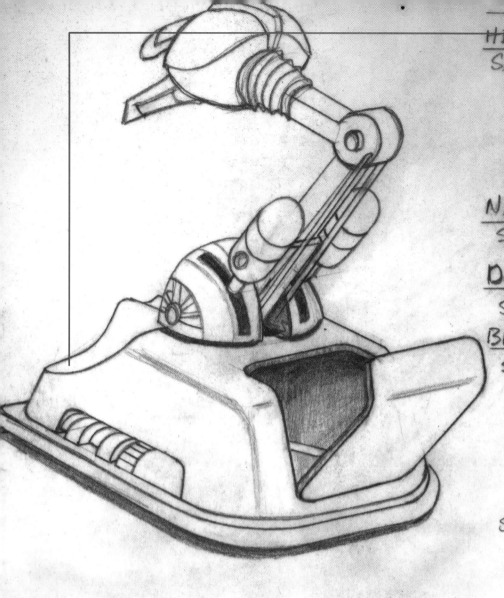

HEAD.
SERVOS 1 Open/Close Claws
2 Rock - Side to Side
3 Rock - To + Fro.
4 Pop Up Eyes (20°

NECK
SERVOS 1 Sail 10kg Torque

DOME
SERVO 1 Rotation 360°

BASE
SERVOS 1 Forward.
2 Steering.
3 Hatch
4 Indicators

SERVO TOTAL (11)
2 Transmitters.
Max 7 Channels each

FINISH
Semi - Gloss Blue
HEAD Lights Red
Static or Flashing?
Brake Lights
Flashing - Variable.

× 3014

BILL PEARSON

# PART ONE.

## TITLES

### 1 EXT. CGI/MODEL SEQUENCE

Red Dwarf in space.

### 2 INT. CORRIDOR - DAY

The sound of marching. Lister and Rimmer, round a corner, followed by two guards and are marched into:

### 3 INT. CAPTAIN'S OFFICE

Rimmer salutes. Lister waves. Ackerman stands to one side.

**HOLLISTER**
I understand you played an idiotic prank on a senior and much respected officer yesterday?

**RIMMER**
That is just not true, sir. We played the prank on Mr Ackerman, sir. We ... (**realizes**) oh, I see.

**HOLLISTER**
What happened?

**LISTER**
We inserted a capsule of the truth serum, sodium pentothal, into his asthma inhaler, sir.

**HOLLISTER**
Which is why he rushed onto the bridge this morning, apologised for being late, saying he'd been having jiggy jiggy with the Science Officer's wife and hadn't allowed enough time to change out of his Batman outfit.

**RIMMER**
Permission to snigger, sir.

**HOLLISTER**
Permission refused.

**RIMMER**
May have to snigger anyway, sir.

Rimmer and Lister both snigger.

**HOLLISTER**
Do either of you have anything to say?

**LISTER**
About what, sir?

**HOLLISTER**
About Mr Ackerman. About him being late and

wearing a Batman outfit.

**LISTER**
Has he considered being Tarzan? The costume change would be much quicker.

**HOLLISTER**
You two are both serving a two-year sentence in the brig - do you want to get out - ever?

**LISTER**
It's just Mr Ackerman is so horrible, sir.

**ACKERMAN**
I am not, sir. I'm extremely nice, lovely in fact, warm, caring, but most of all nice - hence my nick-name, 'Nicey Ackerman'. That's why I entered the service, sir, so I could share my sunny disposition with inmate scum who didn't have my start in life.

**RIMMER**
Sir, he's been horrible from the moment we first met him. ~~Permission for a flash back, sir.~~

**HOLLISTER**
~~Make it quick.~~

### 4 INT. PARADE GROUND IN FACTORY - DAY

The gang and a group of deranged inmates, humans, droids, mixed sexes, stand to attention.

**ACKERMAN**
Today, we have a new intake. To them I say: obey the rules, keep out of trouble, and your time here will pass much more pleasantly. Welcome to Floor 13.

**CAT**
(**To Lister**) Seems like a nice guy.

Ackerman beats the Cat to a pulp with his stick.

Cat gets to his feet.

**ACKERMAN**
If you want to speak, ask my permission.

**CAT**
I was saying how nice you seemed.

**ACKERMAN**
You spoke again.

**Warden Knot and guard join in, and beat him to a second pulp. He gets to his feet again.**

**CAT**
But I was paying you a compliment, buddy: I was saying how you seemed to be a fair-minded, OK, kind of guy. Not one of these psycho types you sometimes get, who run prisons.

**ACKERMAN**
You spoke again.

**More blows from Knot, guard and Ackerman.**

**CAT**
Isn't anyone gonna back me up?

**The others stand to attention, silent and angelic looking.**

**CAT**
(During beating) Hang on, wait, I get it, I should shut up. If I shut up they'll stop hitting me.

**Silence. They stop. He gets up again.**

**CAT**
That is definitely the key.

**He gets beaten again.**

~~**CAT**~~
~~(Proudly) What did I tell you?~~

## 5 INT. CAPTAIN'S OFFICE - DAY

**As we were. Hollister, Ackerman, Lister and Rimmer.**

**ACKERMAN**
That is totally untrue, sir. What actually happened ...

**HOLLISTER**
Save it, save it, Mr Ackerman. I've thought long and hard about a suitable punishment and I've come up with this. You and a team of your choice will play basketball against a team of guards, led by Mr Ackerman.

**ACKERMAN**
God bless you, sir.

**HOLLISTER**
Where you will be trounced and humiliated in front of the entire inmate population.

**RIMMER**
But, sir, if we lose, Baxter and his cronies will beat us to a pulp.

**HOLLISTER**
You better win then.

## 6 INT. BASKET BALL COURT - DAY

**Guards 48 - Cons 3.**
**The posse are playing against the guards, including Hollister, and are getting whooped big time - sounds of disappointed crowd. Guards score another basket and we see the score. Posse getting beaten up by guards.**

**There's a time-out.**

**HOLLISTER**
OK guys, way to go!

**KRYTEN**
Where were you?

**KOCHANSKI**
Where was I?

**KRYTEN**
You were supposed to be picking up Rice.

**KOCHANSKI**
I did. We're meeting for drinks on Thursday.

**KRYTEN**
Not that kind of picking up, you ninny.

**KOCHANSKI**
Look, if I flirt with him a lot, he's going to be distracted and not score so many baskets. And don't start picking on me. I scored all our points.

**KRYTEN**
That last one didn't count. There was a melee and you scored with my head.

**CAT**
Buddies, we gotta stop arguing - we can't lose this.

**LISTER**
We've got it all taken care of.

**RIMMER**
Soon as the guards swig their half-time juice.

**LISTER**
Yeah, the Skutters managed to smuggle something out of the Medi-lab for us. You know that stuff that helps impotent guys put the zest back in their love lives?

**KRYTEN**
'Boing', the virility enhancement drug?

**LISTER**
That's the stuff. We've Mickey Finned their drinks.

**RIMMER**
Within seconds you're harder than a quadratic equation and it doesn't wear off for seven hours.

**KRYTEN**
For seven hours those guys are going to be like catapults. That's going to seriously slow them down.

**CAT**
You're not kidding. Try moving fast with a fishing pole in your pants.

**Guards including Ackerman drink juice.**

**HOLLISTER**
Get out there and kill. They're lambs to the slaughter. Go on, get them!

**Ackerman and guards suddenly become aware a visitor has arrived in their trousers.**

**Time-out over, embarrassed guards hobble as best they can onto the pitch.**

Montage of rest of basketball game: guards can't run properly and only catch with one hand, the other being strategically placed over the groinal area. They get hammered by the posse.

**HOLLISTER**
Come on, get your hands up!

**HOLLISTER**
Get your hands up, don't let them shoot!

Hollister watches from the side line, absently drinks juice. As the drink takes effect he concertinas downwards out of shot and hobbles off.

## 7 INT. CORRIDOR - DAY

Empty corridor. Sound of marching. From round a corner Lister and Rimmer come into view being marched down the corridor by two guards, clearly in deep smeg.

## 8 INT. HOLLISTER'S QUARTERS - DAY

Rimmer salutes, Lister waves.

**HOLLISTER**
Seven hours! Do you know how long that is? I couldn't remove my shorts until after midnight. When I wanted a leak I had to do a hand-stand on the toilet seat. I stopped the lift doors from closing and I wasn't even catching a lift. I caught the shuttle to the all night hospital. I had to pay two fares. Where'd you get it, the Medi-lab?

**LISTER**
Yes, sir.

**HOLLISTER**
How? If it was one of those damned Skutters I'm going to have it crushed.

**LISTER**
It was, uh, me, sir, when the Doc's back was turned. I went up to the Medi-lab for a sick note but the Doc thought I was feigning illness and didn't accept it was possible to have athlete's hand.

**HOLLISTER**
First thing tomorrow, you're on spud duty for two weeks. Now get out of my sight, both of you's.

**RIMMER**
Not spud duty!

**LISTER**
Not with my athlete's hand.

**HOLLISTER**
Out!

## 9 INT. CGI SEQUENCE

Prison establisher.

## 10 INT. PRISON QUARTERS – EVENING

**Rimmer is playing draughts with himself. Lister is doing a puzzle book, frowning.**

**RIMMER**
Stuck?

**LISTER**
Yeah. God this is hard.

**RIMMER**
What you doing –
a crossword?

**LISTER**
No, join the dots.

**RIMMER**
What number are you
stuck on?

**LISTER**
124.

**RIMMER**
124? 124? **(Snaps fingers)**

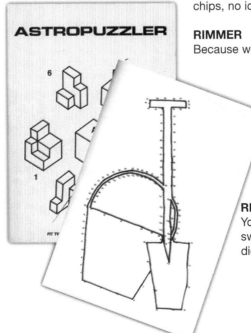

Have you tried 125?

**LISTER**
I know the number, you gimboid, it's finding it that's the hard bit. I'm not some brain-dead simpleton. Ah, there it is. Oh, look at that: It's a bucket and spade.

**Lister holds it up.**

**LISTER**
It's clever that, isn't it?

**Guard enters with supper on a tray.**

**RIMMER**
Ah, supper.

**Guard puts meal on table and makes to exit.**

**RIMMER**
**(Sotto to Lister)** Are we supposed to tip them? I'm never sure.

**Guard exits.**

**Rimmer takes off lid and grimaces at the smell.**

**RIMMER**
I've seen things more appetizing on the floors of elephant houses. Only a total idiot would eat this. **(He starts to eat)** They call this meat? My grand-mother's buttocks deep fried in old chip fat would taste better than this.

**LISTER**
We're on the punishment menu now. No chips, no ice cream, just the basics.

**RIMMER**
Because we're on punishment detail?

**LISTER**
Yeah, Kill Crazy reckons they give us the cloning experiments that have gone wrong, with some gravy slopped over to disguise it.

**RIMMER**
You waited until I was swallowing till you said that, didn't you?

**LISTER**
He swears blind the other day he got something with two noses in it.

**RIMMER**
Of course, he didn't. They can't do that, it's illegal.

**LISTER**
His starter sneezed, Jimbo Steele was a witness.

**RIMMER**
Kill Crazy's insane. He's got lots of strange ideas. He reckons every time they flush a loo on a plane it drops straight out. And that's why they don't let you go to the lav when the plane's standing on the runway, for fear of skid starts.

**LISTER**
He's probably right.

**RIMMER**
Course he isn't.

**LISTER**
Why else won't they let you go then?

**RIMMER**
I don't know. Maybe they're helping you break up your journey. If they let you go to the loo first off you'll have nothing to do after you've eaten your cheese.

**LISTER**
No, Kill Crazy's probably right. That's why houses on the flight path are always so cheap.

**RIMMER**
Because of all the flushing planes?

**LISTER**
Yeah, well, think about it. You can't sunbathe, you can't have a barbecue, and every time you go out you have to wear a washable hat and leg it to your car.

**RIMMER**
It's the noise. That's why houses on the flight path are so cheap, because of the noise.

**LISTER**
The noise?

**RIMMER**
Yeah.

**LISTER**
But they're half a mile up. You'd never be able to hear people on the loo from that distance. Well, not unless they were like my Uncle Dan.

~~**RIMMER**~~
~~The noise of the planes, you twonk!~~

**RIMMER**
Not eating?

**LISTER**
Yeah, in a minute.

**A tapping noise. Lister opens hatch in roof. Skutter appears holding a silver curry container. Lister opens container and smells.**

**LISTER**
Oh, chicken vindaloo. Nice one, Bob.

**Skutter retreats into its housing again and produces a six-pack of lager.**

**Rimmer watches astounded.**

**LISTER**
What about the poppadums. You didn't forget them, did you?

**Bob ducks back into his housing and produces 3 pops in paper bag. Lister takes one out and takes a bite.**

**LISTER**
(Chewing) Poppadums. Here's a little something for you.

**Lister sprays Bob with some WD40. Bob emits a Skuttery sigh of pleasure.**

**LISTER**
Same time tomorrow.

**Bob nods and exits. Lister starts to eat as Rimmer gawps in amazement. Lister starts to drink.**

**LISTER**
Cheers.

**RIMMER**
Is that the Skutter who got you the stiffening solution for the basket-ball game?

**LISTER**
Yeah, he can get anything, can Bob. A claw in every pie.

**RIMMER**
Tomorrow, we're on spud duty and those knives are supposed to be as sharp as a chemistry teacher's cardigan. Do you reckon he can get us a couple of good potato peelers?

**LISTER**
Hang on, I'm onto something here. Forget the potato peelers, what we want is one of those programmable viruses from the science block.

**RIMMER**
Programmable what?

**LISTER**
Yeah, they used to be on Z Deck. I wonder if the nanos have reconstructed them. You can program them to do anything you want, eat potato skins, you name it.

**RIMMER**
So we could program them to eat the skins off the potatoes and leave the rest intact?

**LISTER**
We wouldn't have to lift a finger.

**RIMMER**
Two weeks of hell would become potato paradise.

**LISTER**
I'll get on the blower to Bob's missus. She'll take a message for us.

**RIMMER**
Bob's got a missus?

**LISTER**
Yeah, Madge. She's amazing, 0-60 in under ten minutes.

**Lister starts tapping out some morse code sounding noises on the pipes with his metal fork.**

**There is a pause, then a reply.
Lister answers with more beats.**

**There is another reply of still more beats. In fact, this could probably go on for a very long time. Finally.**

**LISTER**
Damn.

**RIMMER**
Can't he help us?

**LISTER**
No, wrong number. I got the Chinese laundry. Do you need anything ironing?

**Lister grins. He's taking the smeg.**

**11 EXT. MODEL SEQUENCE**

**A new Canaries transport craft flies towards a mysterious-looking ship.**

**Caption: 'Destination SS *Manny Celeste*:- mission locate Canary battalion, radio contact lost at 4.53am.'**

**12 INT. SPOOKY CORRIDOR ABOARD MYSTERIOUS SHIP – DAY**

**Five Canaries plus Kryten, Kochanski and the Cat creep down the corridor. Canaries split one way, our lot another. Tight shot of Kryten.**

**KRYTEN**

Now, remember - two entire battalions went missing from this ship. Vanished without trace. We must stick together and remain constantly vigilant.

We cut wide and see he is totally alone now.

**KRYTEN**

One minute everything's fine, then you lose concentration for a split second, and you're all alone and easy pickings for some hostile life-form. I know you think I'm a bit of a fusspot when it comes to safety procedures but it's staying alert that has kept us all ...

He looks around.

**KRYTEN**

... kept us ... (He tries to shout quietly) Hello!!?

No reply.

**KRYTEN**

Oh, Creator, I'm on my own.

Cat pokes his head out of a door.

**CAT**

Hey, Buddy! We're in here.

## 13 INT. CHAMBER - DAY

Kryten goes into the chamber.

**KRYTEN**

What is the point of me giving my 'stay alert everyone' pep talk if no-one is listening.

**CAT**

(Not listening) What?

A Canary battalion stands frozen in time.

**KOCHANSKI**

Look at this.

Kochanski releases Holly onto a wall.

**KOCHANSKI**

What are they, Hol?

**HOLLY**

They look uncannily like something you should be very, very afraid of.

**CAT**

What?

**HOLLY**

Mime artists. The ones you get in those trendy town centres that chase you down the street and freeze when you look at them and everyone laughs at you.

**KOCHANSKI**

Oh, I hate them, they're so annoying. They always follow you when you're shopping and mime they want a date and you say 'no' but they won't go away and you end up having to cower in the loo in some really chic Italian shoe shop. Then when you come out, they're still there, so in the end you have to give them a fake phone number. I hate having to do that, don't you?

**HOLLY**

I'm so glad it's not just me that stuff happens to.

Kryten scans the figures with a PSI scan.

**KRYTEN**

I've never seen anything like this before. A group of men who display all the normal life-signs but seem totally incapable of movement.

**HOLLY**

Never seen QPR play away then?

One of the figures is holding a remote device in his hand. Kochanski gently removes it.

**KOCHANSKI**

Tempus. That's Latin. For time.

**CAT**

Latin? I didn't even know the Romans built space ships.

**KRYTEN**

Somehow this device appears to have caused time to freeze. Obviously they used it erroneously.

Kryten turns it the right way round and stabs some buttons. There is a weird CGI effect and the Canaries start to move.

**MEX**

Where did y-ou come from? And how di-d you get hold of that? It's some kind of temp-oral stor-age unit.

They freeze again.

**KRYTEN**

Extraordinary.

**CAT**
Hey ... this could be a great device for settling arguments.

**MEX**
Don't mess wi-th that thing. It can rea-lly scre-e-e-e-e-ew you u-p. ~~Look what happened to me? Do I lo-ok like some kind ma-jor pra-a-a-att or what?~~

**KRYTEN**
It appears to be able to digitize time and then download it and store it on a hard drive. This pure time can then be uploaded into objects or places ...

**KOCHANSKI**
To freeze people?

**KRYTEN**
Technically, they're not frozen, ma'am, merely operating in a different time stream.

**KOCHANSKI**
So you mean they're moving - just incredibly slowly?

**HOLLY**
About the same speed as the average Little Chef waitress. That's why they don't appear to be actually doing anything.

**KOCHANSKI**
So this device has the ability to make time come to a complete stop?

~~**CAT**~~
~~Sounds like one of Goalpost Head's anecdotes.~~

**KOCHANSKI**
What else can it do?

**As Kryten examines the device another time jet hits Kochanski and the Cat and they are instantly replaced by two six-year-old versions of themselves.**

**SIX-YEAR-OLD KOCHANSKI**
What's happened? Kryten, why are you so big and why do I suddenly feel like a Vimto?

**SIX-YEAR-OLD CAT**
Waaa - you've gotta get me back to normal.

**SIX-YEAR-OLD KOCHANSKI**
Do something. I can't go back like this!

**KRYTEN**
Why not? You may only be three feet tall but you're both as cute as buttons.

**Kryten extends his arm, points Tempus and a grown-up Kochanski and grown-up Cat appear. She has long hair down to her bum; he has afro.**

**KOCHANSKI**
What's happened to my hair?

**CAT**
And what's happened to mine?

**HOLLY**
You look like the Turkish entry in the Eurovision Song Contest.

**KRYTEN**
It seems to have restored your hair to a previous time period to the rest of you. Compensating ... (**Recalibrating furiously**)

**He points and fires again. Now Kochanski is wearing a costume from her late teens, something stupid, and so is the Cat.**

**KRYTEN**
Now it's regressed your outfits to a previous time in your lives.

**HOLLY**
And you still look like the Turkish entry in the Eurovision Song Contest.

~~CAT~~
(To Koch) Nice oufit, you look like ~~Lady Godiva~~ let loose in an Oxfam shop.

**~~KRYTEN~~**
~~I'll try again....~~

Kryten returns them to normal.

**KOCHANSKI**
So here's the question: can you unfreeze these guys but take them back in time so they have no memory of finding this?

**KRYTEN**
I think so, ma'am. Why?

**KOCHANSKI**
If we can smuggle this thing back on Red Dwarf, it can make our prison terms pass in seconds.

~~CAT~~
~~Plus we can save a fortune in laundry bills.~~

**KRYTEN**
Leave this to me. I have an excellent place to conceal it.

## 14  INT.  SECURITY - DAY

The various Canaries go through, have their guns confiscated and get patted down. Kochanski, Cat are cleared. Kryten starts to get patted down too. His head is unusually high - it's not a mystery where the time wand is.

## 15  INT.  CORRIDOR - DAY

Bob the Skutter holding a vial of the virus goes down the corridor and palms the vial to Lister, who is walking along with Rimmer and two guards.

**LISTER**
Nice one, Bob.

## 16  INT.  POTATO ROOM - DAY

CGI potato mountain.

They stand before an enormous mountain of potatoes. Lister releases the virus. They wait, seemingly nothing happening.

## 17  BEHIND POTATO MOUNTAIN

**RIMMER**
It's not working, is it?

**LISTER**
Give it a bit of time to get going.

**Then suddenly.**

**RIMMER**
Look, look. It's working on this one. And here's another. And another. And another.

**Rimmer holds up the peeled potatoes in triumph.**

**RIMMER**
Fan-smegging-tastic, Listy. We're on our way. They're going to do the whole damn room in minutes.

**We see that half of Rimmer's sleeve is missing.**

**LISTER**
Hey, what's happened to your sleeve, man?

**RIMMER**
What?

**LISTER**
Your sleeve? I didn't notice that before.

**RIMMER**
My God, they're eating my clothes.

Rimmer jumps about trying to knock the virus off his clothes which continue to be eaten away. Soon he's half naked.

Lister watches, laughing. Soon Rimmer's hair starts to disappear too. Lister is doubled up laughing but we see his sleeve and trousers are being eaten away too. Suddenly he realizes and starts doing the same 'get this virus off me' dance as Rimmer.

## 18  INT.  CORRIDOR - DAY

As before, empty corridor, sound of marching. Lister and Rimmer come into shot, marching between two guards. They are both naked and totally bald.

## 19  INT.  CAPTAIN'S QUARTERS - DAY

Hollister stands furious.

**HOLLISTER**
Well?

**RIMMER**
It wasn't me, sir. It was him. He made me do it.

**LISTER**
You Judas. I thought we'd agreed to refuse
to talk.

**RIMMER**
Just let me blame you first, then I'll refuse to talk.

**HOLLISTER**
If I ever, EVER, see you in this
office again, then you're in the
hole. Is that what you want?

**LISTER/RIMMER**
No, sir.

**HOLLISTER**
Well then, get out.

**RIMMER**
Thank you, sir.

**Rimmer shakes his hand.**

**RIMMER**
Thank you.

**Hollister looks at his sleeve which
starts to be
eaten away.**

**HOLLISTER**
You haven't been down to the Medi-bay to get
this virus off, have you?

**RIMMER**
I probably shouldn't have shaken your hand, sir,
that was probably a mistake.

**LISTER**
A big mistake, sir.

**RIMMER**
I, uh, we'll be going, sir.

**LISTER**
Right now.

**Hollister feels his hair, he's nearly
bald too.**

**HOLLISTER**
That's it. Two months. In the hole!!

**LISTER**
Sir, what about my athlete's hand?

**Hollister is now totally bald.**

**HOLLISTER**
Now!!

## 20 INT. CANARIES' MESS HALL ABOARD NEW TRANSPORT CRAFT - DAY

Kryten, now normal head size, stands in line with the Cat and Kochanski waiting to be served.

**KRYTEN**
Straight after lunch, we zap the ship with a two-year download of time and the records will show that we've served our sentences and are free to be released.

**KOCHANSKI**
This machine's amazing. Do you think it can do boob jobs too. Obviously, I'm just thinking about the future.

Baxter takes tray, one in front of Cat. Cat takes tray. Cat backs into him.

**BAXTER**
You spilt my soup.

**CAT**
Sorry, Baxter, non-bud, it was an accident.

Baxter puts Cat's head in dispensing machine.

**BAXTER**
(Growls) Hot Bovril.

**CAT**
Huh? Aaaahhh!

Baxter yanks the Cat's head out of the dispensing machine, grabs Cat's finger and uses it to punch in code for another meal, takes his meal and Cat's meal and heads for the canteen.

~~**CAT**~~
~~That's all my food.~~

## 21 INT. CANTEEN - DAY

Baxter sits with crony, simultaneously eating his two trays of food. Kochanski (with her food), Cat, and Kryten sit down.

**KRYTEN**
Look at him, the big lug. I'd hate to clean the bath out after him. You'd need a sander to get rid of the tide mark and a leaf vac to hoover the hair.

**CAT**
(To Kryten) Fix him. Fix him with the time wand.

~~**KRYTEN**~~
What's for lunch?

~~**KOCHANSKI**~~
~~Chicken, potatoes and carrots - why?~~

**KRYTEN**
Watch this.

Kryten points Tempus discreetly at Baxter - and presses a button.

A jet of time hits Baxter's plate. The meal turns into a live chicken whi~~ch walks off his plate.~~

Baxter hits one man sitting next to him who's laughing. All laughter dies down except for Cat's. Baxter and his buddy get up.

~~**BAXTER**~~
(To Cat) What you laughing at?

**CAT**
They just told me a joke.

**BAXTER**
What joke?

~~**CAT**~~
~~Why did the chicken cross the plate.~~

Baxter launches himself at the Cat. Kryten levels the time wand and freezes Baxter in mid air - all Canaries look amazed, Kryten freezes them too.

~~Kryten stands, spins Baxter in the direction he~~ came from.

**KRYTEN**
What goes around comes around.

Kryten releases another time jet.

Baxter fires across the canteen landing on the table and crushing his crony. All canaries re-animate. Baxter gets up and backs off.

**BAXTER**
We don't want no 'gro. Have your grub back, man. Mutual respect.

Kryten zaps him again. Baxter stands there dressed like a baby. Bonnet, nappy, cardy.

**CAT**
Tell you what, hand over the food and I'll burp ~~you. What d'you say, dummy?~~

~~Cat takes food.~~

**KRYTEN**
(To Cat) Food wise I think we can do rather better than this, sir. Allow me to illustrate.

~~Kryten freezes Baxter and Co. Cat, Kryten & Kochanski exit.~~

## 22 INT. THE HOLE – DAY

It's very dark and dank. The door opens and Lister and Rimmer are flung inside, obviously still bald.

**RIMMER**
Two months, two months stuck in here with you. You think if I appeal they might be compassionate and give me the death sentence instead.

**LISTER**
Look, we're going to be fine.

**RIMMER**
How we going to pass the time?

**LISTER**
By talking.

**RIMMER**
For two months?

**LISTER**
We'll take turns choosing a subject and give talks to one another about themes and topics we're interested in.

**RIMMER**
Oh great, I'm going to become an expert in how to play the rock classics with a kazoo lodged between my buttocks.

From out of the darkness, Bird Man, a demented old man, says ...

**BIRD MAN**
Hello.

**LISTER**
Hey, there's somebody in here with us.

**BIRD MAN**
Yeah, it's that bloke sitting next to you.

**LISTER**
Who are you? What's your name?

**BIRD MAN**
They call me Bird Man.

**LISTER**
Oh aye, why's that?

**RIMMER**
Because he really likes instant custard - why do you think?

Bird Man strokes a little sparrow in his hands.

**BIRD MAN**
This is Pete.

Pete does a little sparrow sneeze. He's got a cold.

**BIRD MAN**
He's nine years old which in sparrow years is ... nine years old. So that makes him ...

**RIMMER**
... nine?

**BIRD MAN**
Nine, that's right. You met him before, have you?

**RIMMER**
Two months of this, God.

Suddenly a red line appears on the floor which traces a circle on the ground.

**RIMMER**
What's this?

The circle of steel is pushed up and slid across and Bob's head appears out of the hole. He whistles the theme from *The Great Escape*, then signals for Lister, Rimmer and Bird Man to follow.

~~**RIMMER**~~
~~I'm not going.~~

**LISTER**
Why not?

**RIMMER**
Because we'll get caught. And if we get caught we're finished.

**LISTER**
Please yourself.

**RIMMER**
I'm not moving. I'm staying here. I'm being a good boy. I think I might tidy up the cell, arrange the rat droppings in alphabetical order or something, or better still write a nice poem about Captain Hollister.

Lister and Bird Man go.

**LISTER**
There was a nice captain called Hollister who ... nothing rhymes with Hollister. Smeg.

Rimmer escapes too.

## 23 INT. CORRIDOR - DAY

The air vent shaft leads into a corridor. Lister, Rimmer and Bob crawl into corridor.

## 24 INT. GAMES ROOM

Other prisoners frozen in time. Two frozen men playing ping-pong.

**RIMMER**
What happened to everyone?

**LISTER**
It's like they're all frozen on the spot.

**RIMMER**
Yvonne McGruder went like this when I tried to kiss her.

**LISTER**
Hey-hey, this will drive them crazy.

Lister takes the ping-pong ball.

## 25 INT. VAST CARGO BAY - DAY

Bob, Lister, Rimmer and Bird Man walk into a vast cargo bay. In the middle, a table is set for dinner and Kryten, Kochanski and the Cat sit around drinking wine, wearing 'time' clothes.

**KOCHANSKI**
Hey!

**LISTER**
Guys.

**KRYTEN**
Sirs!

**CAT**
Buddies.

**RIMMER**
This is Bird Man.

**BIRD MAN**
And this is Pete.

Pete does another little sparrow sneeze.

They sit and start to eat.

**KOCHANSKI**
We found this machine that can digitize time and we can release jets of it and we reckon it can make our sentence pass in a nano second.

**KRYTEN**
Hats off, sirs.

Kryten sends a time jet at Lister and Rimmer which restores their hair.

**BIRD MAN**
There's something wrong with Pete.

**LISTER**
What?

**BIRD MAN**
He's gone all stiff.

**RIMMER**
He must have drunk the guards' half-time juice.

**LISTER**
Not that kind of stiff, he's dead.

**BIRD MAN**
The excitement of being free has killed him.

Lister and Kryten and Rimmer and Kochanski and Cat huddle.

**LISTER**
He really loved that bird. It's the only thing that kept him going.

**KRYTEN**
I can't guarantee anything, sir, but I think the time wand could bring Pete back to life. Make him young and strong again. Watch ...

Kryten points time wand at cage. The cage explodes into two halves which clang onto the floor. Bird Man's glasses fall to the floor. A huge, scaly foot slams onto the ground. Everyone looks up. Except for Bird Man who tries to find his glasses. Large Dino looms above them and roars.

**LISTER**
Holy ...

**RIMMER**
... smeg!

**LISTER**
Where the hell did Barney's ugly brother come from?

**KRYTEN**
From Pete, sir. Birds are descended from dinosaurs, from the theropod family. I inadvertently reversed evolution several million years.

**CAT**
There's an old cat saying, which has particular relevance here. It goes something like this: 'We are all gonna die!'

Bird Man still can't find his glasses.

**BIRD MAN**
(Peering at foot) Pete? Is that you, Pete?

**KOCHANSKI**
Bird Man!

Bird Man finds his glasses and backs off before looking up at Pete, the dino does a gigantic dino sneeze and covers Bird Man in dino sneezy gloop.

**RIMMER**
Gesundheit.

Bird Man reaches into his pocket and holds something up.

**BIRD MAN**
You want some seed?

Dino P.O.V. shot as Dino Pete swoops down onto Bird Man and swallows him whole.

Bird man's boots stick out of Pete's mouth.

**BIRD MAN**
(Echoey) That's a no then, is it?

There is a crunch and the boots land on the floor minus their owner.

**KRYTEN**
What now, sir?

**RIMMER**
Follow the Rimmer shaped blur.

Static shot. Rimmer exits left, the others exit right. There is a pause before Rimmer flies back across shot in hot pursuit.

The T-Rex starts to follow as the group head for a matrix of wooden crates.

CAPTION: 'TO BE CONTINUED'.

## TITLES

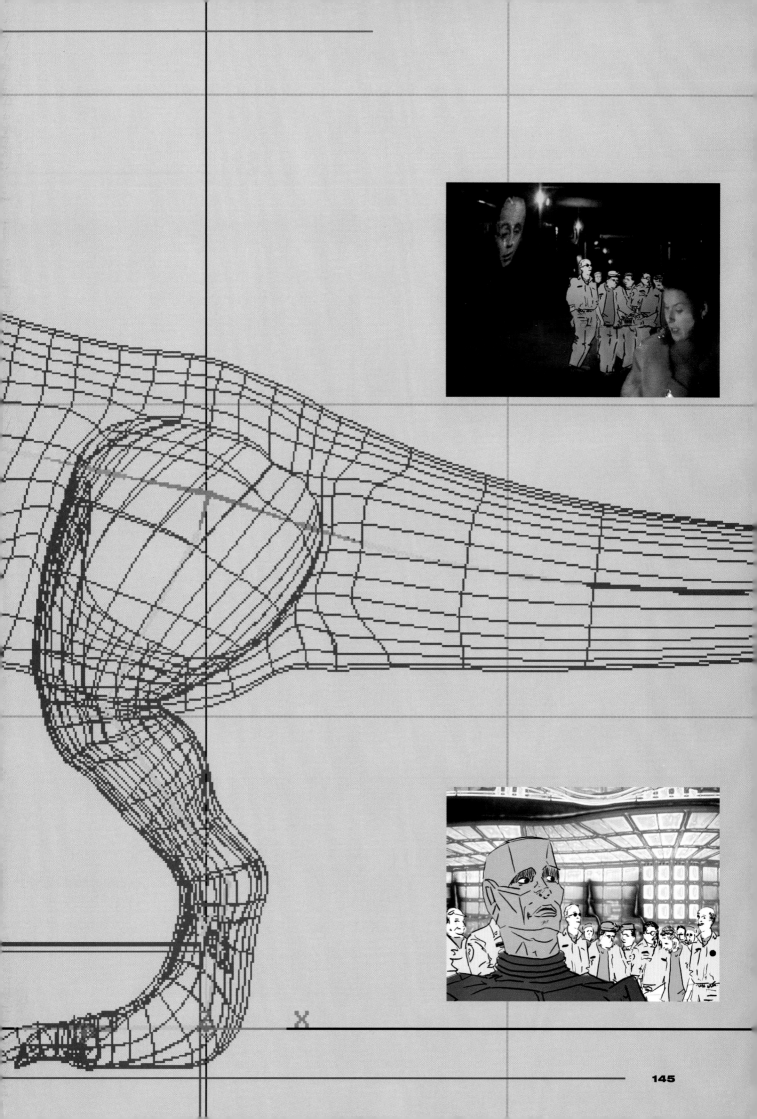

# PART ONE.

## Cast & Crew

Written by: **DOUG** NAYLOR

Rimmer: **CHRIS** BARRIE  Lister: **CRAIG** CHARLES  Cat: **DANNY** JOHN-JULES

Kryten: **ROBERT** LLEWELLYN  Kochanski: **CHLOË** ANNETT  Holly: **NORMAN** LOVETT

Hollister: **MAC** McDONALD  Ackerman: **GRAHAM** McTAVISH  Mex: **ANDREW** ALSTON

Young Kochanski: **HOLLY** EARL  Young Cat: **PERRI** MICHAEL  Baxter: **RICKY** GROVER

Birdman: **IAN** MASTERS  Warden Knot: **SHEND**


Casting Director: **LINDA** GLOVER  Music: **HOWARD** GOODALL

Production Accountant: **MIKE** AMOS  Graphic Designer: **ANDY** SPENCE

General Manager GNP LTD: **HELEN** NORMAN  Location Manager: **KEN** HAWKINS

Production Co-ordinator: **RACHEL** STEWART

Post-Production Co-ordinator: **SIMON** BURCHELL

Stage Manager: **JACQUELINE** ZOPPI-TIGHE  Gaffer: **JOHN** BARKER

Props Master: **PAUL** DE CSERNATONY  Props Buyer: **TIM** YOUNGMAN

Art Director: **IAN** READE-HILL  Vision Mixer: **JOHN** BARCLAY

Engineering Manager: **ALAN** GODLEMAN  Camera Operator: **ANDY** MARTIN

Location Sound: **NIGEL** DAVIS  Sound Supervisor: **JEM** WHIPPEY  **Geoff** Moss

Editor: **MARK** WYBOURN  Script Associate: **PAUL** ALEXANDER

Script Supervisor: **GILLIAN** WOOD  First Assistant Director: **JULIE** SYKES

Visual Effects Designer: **JIM** FRANCIS  **Ed** Smith  **Mark** Howard

Digital Effects Designer: **CHRIS** VEALE  Make Up Designer: **ANDREA** FINCH

Costume Designer: **HOWARD** BURDEN  Line Producer: **JO** BENNETT

Production Designer: **MEL** BIBBY  Director of Photography: **PETER** MORGAN

Executive Producer: **DOUG** NAYLOR  Produced and Directed by: **ED** BYE

# INTRODUCTION
## PETE - PART TWO.

Ed and I stood in the Line Producer's office. It was seven in the morning and she looked serious. 'I've got some news,' she began. 'You're not going to believe it.'
My immediate thought was Danny had turned up on time for a rehearsal but it was even more incredible than that.
'You know how for the last 12 weeks I've been telling you we were in big big trouble money-wise and how we would have to cut back on something? Well, now we really are in big big trouble money-wise and we've got to cut back on something right now.'
We'd run out of money.
We couldn't shoot the end sequence of the script I'd intended to shoot last called 'Earth'. It was to be the final instalment of the series and the second part of 'Only the Good', at the time called 'Every Dog ...'
The final show was supposed to include an out-of-control Dwarf, travelling at a speed close to light, using anti-matter from the parallel universe and causing a meteor-like impact into the planet Earth, caroming through the White House, totalling the Arc de Triomphe, skidding skilfully round the Taj Mahal - Lister: 'Totalling, that would be sacrilege, man' - but winding up causing a tidal wave that totally destroys the future civilization now living happily on Earth.
Rimmer et al were then supposed to fall out of the finally stationary ship and say: 'Sorry, didn't see you there. Sorry.' And we were to fade out with them exchanging insurance details with one of the few survivors.
Not anymore.
For the first time, we're now able to get an accurate costing. This two-minute sequence alone, it turns out, would cost almost £100,000.
£100,000 we don't have.
'So what now?' I ask.
'You're going to have to come up with a new script which ideally doesn't involve spending any money.'
Where had I heard that line before? Series VII was the last time and the time before that? - Series VI, Series V ...
With most shows you have a very good idea exactly how much everything is going to cost before you start. With Red Dwarf, when often you're doing things which haven't been done before on British TV, there's no reference point, so there's no way of knowing until you're half way through.
How much does a dinosaur cost? Can't be answered until you've nearly done it.
With Red Dwarf it's always a bit of a step into the black ...

    A moment of contemplation.
The budget seems to have dogged us every step of the way. The one hour special of 'Back in the Red' had to be turned into three episodes because of money and scheduling.
I'd now lost my final episode and 'Pete' had to become a two-parter instead of the intended single eper.
Only 'Cassandra' and 'Krytie TV' had come out as I intended.
Smeg! Double smeg with lots of smeg on - and then an extra dollop of smeg.
I was not happy.

# RED DWARF VIII

## 'PETE - PART 2'

### EPISODE 7

## Written by
## DOUG NAYLOR
## &
## PAUL ALEXANDER

# PETE PART TWO.

## TITLES

### 1 INT. CARGO BAY - DAY (RECAP OF PT1)

The posse and Bob walk backwards away from Pete.

### 2 INT. CRATES - DAY

The posse scramble behind some crates.

### 3 INT CARGO BAY/CGI SEQUENCE

Pete, the dinosaur, towers over crates.

Kryten runs out trying to be a decoy.

**KRYTEN**
Hey! Pete, eat me.

**KRYTEN**
Here, Bob.

As Pete lunges towards him. Kryten lobs time wand to Bob.

**KRYTEN**
Here, Bob - catch.

Pete follows the flight of the time wand as Bob catches it. He lunges forward and grabs Bob in his mouth.

**LISTER**
Bob!

**KRYTEN**
Bob!

Pete swallows Bob whole.

Lister waits at the cargo bay doors.

**LISTER**
Come on, Kryten, hurry up!

### 4 INT. PETE'S STOMACH - DAY

The camera follows Bob's journey into Pete's stomach. He splashes into the watery depths. There is a long pause before he re-emerges.

### 5 INT. CARGO BAY DOORS - DAY

Kryten just makes it before Lister slams the doors

closed. There is a crash as an imprint of Pete's head smashes into the door. Once ...

Dino head smash again and again.

**KRYTEN**
Leg it mode, sir.

They exit.

### 6 INT. CARGO BAY - BEHIND CRATES

Lister and Kryten arrive.

**LISTER**
We lost the time wand.

**CAT**
How the hell are we gonna get rid of that thing now?

**RIMMER**
WE'RE FINISHED!

**LISTER**
Stop yelling, man, we've got to think our way out of this.

**RIMMER**
(Pause) WE'RE FINISHED!

**LISTER**
Shut up and get a grip, man.

WE'RE FINISHED!

**RIMMER**
(**Composing himself**) I'm sorry, I'm sorry, I'm sorry. It's just I was ... Look, I'm better now. Can I just say one thing?

**LISTER**
Yeah, go on?

**RIMMER**
WE'RE FINISHED!!

**Lister activates Holly.**

**LISTER**
Hol, need some advice, mate. We've been cornered by a T-Rex that was formerly a sparrow. And the only thing that can turn it back into Woody Wood-Pecker is in its stomach. What's your take on the situation?

**HOLLY**
Bye.

**KOCHANSKI**
Kryten?

**KRYTEN**
Yes, ma'am?

**KOCHANSKI**
How long in the normal course of things will it take for Pete to pass the time wand out of his system?

**KRYTEN**
Strangely enough, ma'am, I don't have that information in my database. My programmers, for some insane reason, believed that dinosaur 'bowel movement frequency tables' wouldn't be required. Imbeciles!

**HOLLY**
What do you want, the long or the short version?

**LISTER**
Uh ... long.

**HOLLY**
You're finished.

**CAT**
What's the short version?

**LISTER**
Why, what's your suggestion?

**KOCHANSKI**
Well, the quicker we get the time wand back the better, right?

**LISTER**
Right.

**KOCHANSKI**
Right, so why don't we lure Pete into the Food Bay and get him to eat some roughage.

**CAT**
Get a T-Rex to eat roughage?

**KOCHANSKI**
Yeah, All Bran, prunes, baked beans on toast, that sort of stuff.

**RIMMER**
We can't get Lister to eat that sort of stuff, let alone a seven-ton dinosaur.

**KOCHANSKI**
The more roughage, the quicker we get the time wand back. Have you got any better ideas?

**RIMMER**
Yes. I have got a better idea, actually. I'm going to kill myself.

Massive booms as Pete continues head butting the door.

## 7 INT. CARGO BAY - DAY

As before.

**LISTER**
We've got to keep this dinosaur business quiet or we're dead.

**RIMMER**
Keep him quiet? He's rampaging about the food decks making more noise than two yodelling champions on honeymoon. Everyone on the ship will have heard him by now.

**KRYTEN**
Sir, the crew are frozen operating on a different time stream. If we can recapture the time wand and turn Pete back into a sparrow before the freeze expires, no-one need be any the wiser.

**CAT**
He's right. I just listened to everything he said and I still ain't got a clue what's happening.

## 8 INT. STOMACH - DAY

Bob surfaces, clutching the time wand.
There are some bleepy noises as Bob accidentally presses some of Tempus's buttons.

## 9 INT. TABLE TENNIS AREA - DAY

The table tennis player comes back to life and swings at the ball which is no longer there.

## 10 INT. CARGO BAY - DAY

In the middle sits a large inflatable dinghy which they've turned into a dinosaur bowl.

Cat is driving a fork-lift truck which is carrying a full-sized frozen cow.

**KRYTEN**
(In background) Right over, sir. Come on Mr Cat. Right over.

The bowl is full of a thick brown soup which is bubbling quietly. The Cat lowers the cow into the pool.

## 11 INT. CARGO BAY - BEHIND CRATES - DAY

Rimmer, Lister and Kochanski stand watching.

**RIMMER**
Cow vindaloo. It's not going to work.

**LISTER**
Course it's going to work.

**RIMMER**
T-Rexes don't like curry.

**LISTER**
They're hard, aren't they? Of course they like curries. If a T-Rex was a bloke, he'd be a Geordie - the kind of guy who wears T-shirts in

the middle of winter and his nipples don't even get hard.

**RIMMER**
A seven-ton theropod is not going to eat Indian food. They like flesh, preferably living, liberally coated in blood, with a side order of intestines and an extra portion of blood. They're a bit like the French in that respect.

**LISTER**
Look, we've got nothing to lose. And if the worst comes to the worst and the dino doesn't eat it, I'll scoff it myself. (**Dino makes more dents.**) That door's not going to hold out much longer.

**RIMMER**
If only that damn T-Rex felt like I do now, he wouldn't even need a curry.

## 12 INT. CARGO BAY
The Cat and Kryten are emptying packets of All Bran into the pool.

## 13 INT. CARGO BAY - BEHIND CRATES

**LISTER**
Don't put that stuff in it, you're going to spoil the taste.

**KOCHANSKI**
Here he comes.

They hide.

## 14 INT. BEHIND THE BARRELS - DAY
Pete walks up to the curried swimming pool as the posse hide, watching. It sniffs it, then plunges its head in and starts to eat noisily.

## 15 INT. CARGO BAY BARRELS - DAY
The gang watch.

**LISTER**
It's loving it. Maybe we should have made it some poppadums - you know, gone the whole hog.

**CAT**
The whole hog? Like it wasn't hard enough getting the whole cow.

## 16 CGI SEQUENCE
Pete finishes the curry then lifts it's head up and roars.

## 17 INT. CARGO BAY BARRELS - DAY

**LISTER**
I think it wants a lager.

## 18 ANIMATRONIC SEQUENCE
It looks up, there is a pause, it's eyes widen.

## 19 INT. CARGO BAY BARRELS - DAY

**LISTER**
It was a hot one. With it being a dino I thought it could stand it.

## 20 CGI SEQUENCE
It roars again, this time more plaintively. Then the dinosaur runs around the cargo bay with it's tongue hanging out.

Finally it crashes through a wall into the Food Bay looking for a drink.

## 21 INT. CARGO BAY BARRELS - DAY

**There is the sound of rifles being cocked. The posse look up and see several guards pointing guns at them.**

**KRYTEN**
The time freeze on the guards must have ... if only those buttons were more clearly marked.

## 22 INT. CORRIDOR - DAY

**Empty corridor, sound of marching. From round a corner Lister and Rimmer come into view being marched down the corridor, by same two guards.**

## 23 INT. CAPTAIN'S QUARTERS - DAY

**Lister and Rimmer stand before Hollister whose head is swathed in bandages.**
**Rimmer salutes, Lister waves.**

**HOLLISTER**
The rules on dinosaurs aboard JMC mining ships are very clear. No pets!! Am I right? Am I right?

**LISTER/RIMMER**
Yes, sir.

**HOLLISTER**
Have you any idea the damage that thing has caused?

**LISTER/RIMMER**
No, sir.

**HOLLISTER**
It has eaten our entire supply, two and a half tonnes of mint-choc ice cream. I love mint choc ice-cream and that damn dino has eaten every last bit.

**RIMMER**
We were just trying to get the time wand back, sir.

**HOLLISTER**
It has also eaten four hundred crates of orange ice pops and drank all the Coca-Cola. Guess what?

**LISTER/RIMMER**
You love orange icepops and Coca-Cola, sir.

**HOLLISTER**
I love orange ice pops and Coca-Cola.

**LISTER**
Sir, if you could just let us ...

**HOLLISTER**
You know what happens when a dinosaur eats cow vindaloo and then eats two and a half tonnes of mint-choc ice cream followed by four hundred crates of orange ice pops and swills the whole thing down with 2,000 gallons of a popular fizzy drink? Do you know what happens?

**LISTER**
It burps?

**HOLLISTER**
Oh, it burps. And do you know what happened to the poor brave men who had the misfortune to get in the way of that burp?

**RIMMER**
They went phwoooar? (**Waves away burp**)

**HOLLISTER**
It took out the entire platoon, hurling them twenty feet across the cargo bay wall.

**RIMMER**
Sir, I hope this one small dinosaur incident won't tarnish an otherwise flawless service record, sir.

**HOLLISTER**
Do you know what happens when a dinosaur eats cow vindaloo, two and a half tonnes of mint-choc ice cream, followed by four hundred crates of orange ice pops and swills it all down with 2,000 gallons of a popular fizzy drink, after it's burped?

**RIMMER**
It feels sick.

**HOLLISTER**
Oh no, it doesn't feel sick, Rimmer. It is sick! Five of our best men nearly drowned. Two others are in hospital concussed by pieces of carrot the size of tree trunks.

**LISTER/RIMMER**
We are really, deeply, deeply, deeply sorry, sir.

**HOLLISTER**
Do you know what happens when a dinosaur has eaten cow vindaloo, then eats two and a half tonnes of mint-choc ice cream followed by ...

**LISTER**
Oh God, it didn't!

**HOLLISTER**
It didn't what, Lister?

**LISTER**
It didn't get a diarrhoea attack, did it?

**HOLLISTER**
One hundred per cent correct and do you know what happened to the battalion that was sneaking up on the beast, from behind? Of which I was a proud member? Do you know? Do you know what happened?

**RIMMER**
We've got a fair idea, sir.

**LISTER**
Yes, sir, fair idea, sir.

**HOLLISTER**
A tidal wave. Fifteen feet high. I will be in therapy for the rest of my life. I've had twelve baths and three showers. Now, do you have anything to say?

**RIMMER**
Yes, sir, I think you missed a bit up your left nostril, sir.

**Hollister picks up time wand from his desk.**

**HOLLISTER**
Nobody knows how to work this thing. It is sedated in the cargo bay. Turn it back into a sparrow.

**Hollister gives the time wand to Lister.**

**LISTER**
Sir, what about Bob? Did he show up?

**HOLLISTER**
Who the hell you think landed on my head? He is in repairs being oiled. Bring back the sparrow. And if you try anything smart, you're dead.

**LISTER/RIMMER**
Yes, sir.

**HOLLISTER**
And if I ever, EVER, EVER, see you in this office again, you are finished! (**Looks at his watch**) See you in ten minutes.

**Lister presses time wand.**

**(1) HOLLISTER**
(**Looks at his watch**) See you in ten minutes.

**Lister presses time wand again.**

**(2) HOLLISTER**
(**Looks at his watch**) See you in ten minutes.

**Lister presses time wand again.**

**(3) HOLLISTER**
(**Looks at his watch**) See you in ten minutes.

**Lister presses time wand again.**

**(4) HOLLISTER**
(**Looks at his watch**) See you in ten minutes.

**Lister presses time wand again.**

**(5) HOLLISTER**
(**Looks at his watch**) See you in ten minutes.

## 24 INT. CORRIDOR - DAY

**Kryten and Kochanski walking along corridor.**

**KOCHANSKI**
Did you get punishment duty too?

**KRYTEN**
I've got to iron 800 prison smocks.
I don't understand - why do you get punishment duty and I get a reward. 800 - bliss.

## 25 INT. PRISON QUARTERS - DAY

**Lister and Rimmer enter, they take the Canary case from under the bed and start getting decked out as Canaries.**

**LISTER**
Did you see the Captain's report, the one lying open on his desk? See what it said about you? He used the word 'imbecile' four times in one sentence.

**RIMMER**
Oh yeah. What were the other words in the sentence?

**LISTER**
Just your name and a dash.

**RIMMER**
I don't know. You make a couple of tiny mistakes, you give the Captain a virus that eats all his hair off then you accidentally turn a sparrow into a dinosaur and you never hear the last of it.
He really thinks I'm an imbecile? I'm finished, I'm never going to make it into high command now.

**LISTER**
It's just the people who know you who think you're an imbecile. Everyone else thinks you're a moron.

**Hollister enters. Rimmer unaware. Lister sees him and tries to feed Rimmer a line.**

**LISTER**
He is a good Captain, though, Captain Hollister, isn't he? On the ball, quick.

**RIMMER**
Quick? The only time he's quick is when he's passing a salad bar.

**LISTER**
You do admire him though, don't you?

**RIMMER**
Admire him? A man who has his own cinema pick 'n' mix factory in his quarters? A man who has a walk in fridge? Who lists as his hobbies chewing and swallowing?

**LISTER**
You did tell me once before though you do respect him, don't you?

**RIMMER**
Respect him? A man whose family crest is made up of two cream buns and a profiterole. A man whose idea of a light snack - he's standing behind me, isn't he?

**HOLLISTER**
Yes, he is.

RESPECT HIM? A MAN WHOSE FAMILY C
IS MADE UP OF TWO CREAM BUNS AND
PROFITEROLE. A MAN WHOSE IDEA OF
LIGHT SNACK - HE'S STANDING BEHIN
ISN'T HE?

**RIMMER**
I was just talking about you, sir. I was saying what a big fat lump of blubber I think you are and how that potato virus I contracted yesterday doesn't appear to have had any strange side effects whatsoever. (**Doing weird spasm**) Weeifiiiiii-irrrgh.

**HOLLISTER**
You forgot this.

**Hollister hands them the time wand.**

**HOLLISTER**
You left it in my office. Have you any idea of the damage that this could cause if it got into the wrong hands? Look after it!

**Hollister exits.**

## 26 INT. PRISON QUARTERS – DAY

**Kochanski has a broom and is banging it about under the bunks trying to catch something.**

**KOCHANSKI**
You're there, I know you're there, you little sod. Come on out, out –

**Kryten enters.**

**KOCHANSKI**
There's a mouse under here, it's been scuttling round for about ten minutes.

**KRYTEN**
It's not a mouse, ma'am - it's Archie.

**KOCHANSKI**
Archie?

**KRYTEN**
My penis. It must have escaped.

**KOCHANSKI**
You know I'm really going to have to get my ears syringed, you know what that sounded like to me?

**KRYTEN**
I made one.

**KOCHANSKI**
No forget my ears, maybe my whole brain needs syringing. You made one?

**KRYTEN**
Out of an old electron board, a loo roll, some sticky-back plastic and an Action Man's polo neck jumper.

**KOCHANSKI**
Kryten, why do you want one?

**KRYTEN**
It's so humiliating being posted to the women's wing just because I'm genitally challenged. So I decided to make one like Mr Lister's. The little rascal must have got bored jumping in and out of his hoop and made a break for it during the night.

**KOCHANSKI**
No wonder I couldn't lure him out with a bit of cheese. This whole thing's making sense now.

**KRYTEN**
Just leave this to me, ma'am. Here Archie, here boy. Chu-chu-chu-chu.

**KOCHANSKI**
There he is.

**Kryten throws the waste basket over Archie who rattles around inside the basket before making the waste basket move around the room and out of the door.**

**KOCHANSKI**
Kryten, do you realize what this means?

**KRYTEN**
No ma'am?

**KOCHANSKI**
It means you're a real man.

**KRYTEN**
It does, why?

**KOCHANSKI**
Because now, like all men, you have absolutely no control over your penis.

**KRYTEN**
I'm so proud. (**Calls**) Archie, come back.

**Kryten starts to chase after him.**

**Guard enters with Canary case.**

**GUARD**
All right, girls, new Canary mission.

**KOCHANSKI**
What?

**GUARD**
Untamed dino on the loose.

## 27 CGI SEQUENCE

**Dwarf tube hammers around the ship.**

## 28 INT. TUBE - DAY

**Posse, Kill Crazy, Baxter and others.**

**KOCHANSKI**
We are not going in till we know what we're doing.

**RIMMER**
(Wearily) That could take years.

**KOCHANSKI**
You point that thing at yourself by mistake and you could wind up as a sperm. Is that what you want?

**CAT**
Hell no, none of my suits'll fit.

**KILL CRAZY**
If that gizmo thing don't work, the Captain said we was to go in and have that T-Rex.

**BAXTER**
And we ain't using no guns.

**KILL CRAZY**
No, guns is for woosies. It's gonna be hand-to-hand combat.

**RIMMER**
A fist fight with a T-Rex?

~~**KILL CRAZY**~~
Smegging great!!

**LISTER**
You two, can't get killed quick enough, can you?

**KILL CRAZY**
I'm gonna make a coat out of its skin and have it's feet made into boots.

**CAT**
Sounds good. Have you thought about a ~~matching satchel?~~

~~**KILL CRAZY**~~
Imagine it. (Mimes boxing) Bosh, bosh, pop, pop, bosh.

**BAXTER**
~~I thought you had a glass jaw?~~

**KILL CRAZY**
Yeah, but them T-Rexes, mate, they've only got little arms, haven't they? Ain't got no reach. (Mimes boxing with little arms) I'll just pick it off. Bosh, bosh, bang.

**BAXTER**
It can't reach nothing with those little arms.

**RIMMER**
Probably why they're always a bit grumpy.

~~**KILL CRAZY**~~
All that frustration, yeah.

**BAXTER**
Maybe we could tame it, it'd make a lovely dog.

**KILL CRAZY**
Oi, Dino - 'Sit', 'fetch', 'stop rubbing your arse on that carpet, you filthy beast.
(To Baxter) Imagine taking that down the pub. Girls'd think I was really hard. They might even go out with me then. They might even let me take their bras off.

**BAXTER**
They let some blokes do that, you know.

**KILL CRAZY**
~~Hard blokes.~~

## 29 INT. CARGO BAY - DAY

**The Canaries hammer down some stairs. The posse amongst them.**

**CAT**
Oh, my God.

**KOCHANSKI**
What?

**CAT**
Something's wrong.

**LISTER**
What do you mean, man?

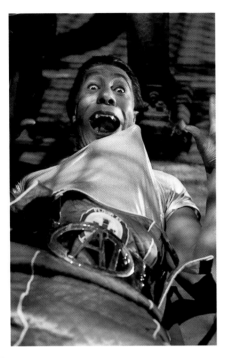

**CAT**
Something's inside me and it wants to get out.

**KOCHANSKI**
Oh, my God.

**CAT**
Aaahhhh! Help! Aaaahh!

Cat collapses to the ground and has a fit, shaking from side to side, on his back, while under his costume, something runs up and down and tries to burst out but doesn't penetrate the material.

**RIMMER**
What is it?

**KRYTEN**
I think it's Archie, sir.

**LISTER**
It's who?

**KOCHANSKI**
It escaped earlier, it must have followed us. It must of dozed off in the Cat's pocket and just woken up.

**LISTER**
Who the smeg is Archie?

**KRYTEN**
Don't be alarmed, sir, it's just my penis is on

the loose.

Cat writhes around on the floor.

**CAT**
Waaaaaaaaa!!!

Lister's walkie talkie buzzes.

**LISTER**
(Into walkie) Yep?

30 INT. OFFICE - DAY

**HOLLISTER**
It's Captain Hollister. How's it going?

31 INT. CARGO BAY - DAY
Cat writhes around still laughing and screaming.

**LISTER**
Very well, sir. Really, really good.

32 INT. OFFICE - DAY

**HOLLISTER**
No more screw-ups, you got that??

**LISTER VOICE**
Absolutely, sir. No more screw-ups.

Hollister hangs up.

33 INT. CARGO BAY - DAY
Kryten grabs Archie in his cupped hands and they put him in a tin. He rattles about furiously inside.

**KRYTEN**
Sorry about that, sir. He's not house-trained yet. He can play dead and beg but that's about it.

**CAT**
We never going to talk about this again, OK? This never happened. OK?

**ALL**
OK.

**KRYTEN**
He was just looking for somewhere warm to go, sir.

**CAT**
He's never heard of a sauna?

## 34 INT. NEW CORRIDOR - DAY

**The posse pad along and turn a corner.**

**Two Canaries grab Lister by the arms. Baxter snatches Tempus.**

**BAXTER**
We want a barny with Barney, don't want any sane people spoiling it.

**KILL CRAZY**
Death or glory. Yee-haaahhhh!

**LISTER**
Hang on guys, come on, wait a minute.

**Baxter zaps Lister and Rimmer with Tempus. Nothing happens. He zaps them again. Still nothing. Baxter tosses it to the floor.**

**BAXTER**
This thing's useless. Say goodbye to your teeth.

**Baxter punches Lister in the face. Another punch. But Lister appears untouched. Kill Crazy punches Rimmer, who again takes it square in the face.**

**LISTER**
Something's not right. We're getting our butts kicked and it doesn't hurt. (**Another punch**) See? Look, I'm not even bleeding.

**Rimmer gets another whack.**

**RIMMER**
You're right.

**Kryten picks up Tempus.**

**KRYTEN**
According to this, sirs, they've put your bodies on a different time stream to the rest of you.

**BAXTER**
Let's go.

**Kill Crazy steals Tempus off Kryten and legs it.**

## 35 INT. CAPTAIN'S OFFICE - DAY

**Rimmer salutes, Lister waves.**

**HOLLISTER**
You lost the time wand?

**LISTER**
We were ambushed,sir.

**HOLLISTER**
By whom?

**LISTER**
Well, first of all by Kryten's ...

**Rimmer shakes head - don't tell him.**

**LISTER**
Then we were jumped by ...

**Again Rimmer interrupts him - don't tell him.**

**LISTER**
Sir.

**HOLLISTER**
That's it? OK, no more Mr Nice Guy. No more second chances. You get that time wand back, you get that sparrow back and if you step out of line one more time, one more time, you're dead! Do you understand?

**Suddenly Lister is yanked out of shot, sails across the room and crashes into a wall smashing through a display.**

**LISTER**
Whu-what was that?

**RIMMER**
I thi-

**Rimmer doubles up in two, he is then hauled into the air and he smashes down onto Hollister's desk removing most of its contents and crashing onto the floor.**

**HOLLISTER**
What the hell is going on?

**RIMMER**
The effects of the fight - they've caught up with us.

Lister and Rimmer receive various blows, which ends with them being thrown head first into Hollister.

**HOLLISTER**
Get out of here, both of you. Out!

They get hurled backwards, still involved in the delayed fight watched by a furious Hollister.

## 36 INT. CARGO BAY TYPE AREA - DAY

Lister and Rimmer creep along.

**LISTER**
Getting that time wand back could take forever. They could zap us with it and turn us into anything.

Rimmer rounds a corner.

**RIMMER**
I don't think getting it back is going to be much of a problem.

Lister turns the corner and sees two chimps dressed in Canary outfits, playing with Tempus.

They take Tempus.

Time cut -

It's gloomy. There is a terrible snoring noise.

**RIMMER**
It's going to go wrong isn't it?

**LISTER**
All I've got to do is press 'undo' and the time wand will retrace its steps and undo everything it's done so far. This way we'll even get Bird Man back.

They peer round the corner. The dino is lying on its back, sleeping.

**RIMMER**
Something's going to go wrong, it always does for us.

**LISTER**
Will you relax!

Lister points the wand and regenerates Bird Man's boots.

**LISTER**
Bird man's boots. Now to get the rest of him back.

**Presses wand again and Lister regenerates Bird Man.**

**BIRD MAN**
Pete ate me. He ate me. He must be really out of sorts. He's never eaten me before. Never.

**Lister points wand at dino and changes him into a sparrow. Bird Man picks him up.**

**BIRD MAN**
Pete, you want some seed?

**RIMMER**
Now destroy the time wand.

**LISTER**
This machine's priceless.

**RIMMER**
Destroy it.

**Lister drops it on the ground and jumps up and down on top of it until it smashes into a thousand pieces.**

**They walk past a giant egg. They freeze.**

**LISTER**
What are we gonna do now?

**RIMMER**
Now, we rebuild the time wand. It's absolutely priceless.

**They try to fix the time wand. There are two more cracking sounds and two dino feet thrust out of the bottom of the egg. The egg takes off across the cargo bay.**

**RIMMER**
Stop that dinosaur!

**The egg runs into the lift. They reach the lift too late as it disappears up into the ship.**

**LISTER**
It's gone in the lift.

**RIMMER**
Get it back! Get it back!

**37  INT. MEDI-BAY - DAY**
Hollister is lying on a massage table. His head in the head hole, getting a massage.

**HOLLISTER**
That coconut milk felt great.

## 38 INT. LIFT - DAY
Lister & Rimmer in lift. Egg shell is empty.

## 39 INT. MEDI-BAY - DAY
Masseuse steps out of the room.

**HOLLISTER**
I'm such a wreck.

## 40 INT. LIFT - DAY
Lister & Rimmer in lift - heads in egg.

## 41 INT. MEDI-BAY - DAY
From under the table we see the baby dino enter and walk up to Hollister and start licking the milk off his back.

**HOLLISTER**
Mmmmm. That's great. There's a certain roughness about your touch that really hits the spot, all sandpapery. Yow - that's good.

## 42 INT. CORRIDOR - DAY
The sound of foot steps. Lister and Rimmer, between two guards, round the corner.

## 43 INT. CAPTAIN'S OFFICE - DAY
Rimmer salutes, Lister waves. Hollister holds up a sign.

'I am suffering from post-traumatic stress disorder.'

Second sign.

'I may never speak again.'

Third sign.

'The hole. Twelve months.'

They start to leave. Hollister writes.

'Where the hell are you going?'

**RIMMER**
The hole, sir.

Hollister writes.

'You're not going to the hole. I am.'

They react.

'See you in twelve months.'

Hollister beams at them triumphantly.

## TITLES

# PETE PART TWO.

## Cast & Crew

Written by: **DOUG** NAYLOR & **PAUL** ALEXANDER

Rimmer: **CHRIS** BARRIE  Lister: **CRAIG** CHARLES  Cat: **DANNY** JOHN-JULES

Kryten: **ROBERT** LLEWELLYN  Kochanski: **CHLOË** ANNETT  Holly: **NORMAN** LOVETT

Hollister: **MAC** McDONALD  Bird Man: **IAN** MASTERS  Kill Crazy: **JAKE** WOOD

Baxter: **RICKY** GROVER


Stunt Co-ordinator: **MARC** CASS  Casting Director: **LINDA** GLOVER

Music: **HOWARD** GOODALL  Production Accountant: **MIKE** AMOS

Graphic Designer: **ANDY** SPENCE  General Manager GNP LTD: **HELEN** NORMAN

Location Manager: **KEN** HAWKINS  Production Co-ordinator: **RACHEL** STEWART

Post-Production Co-ordinator: **SIMON** BURCHELL

Stage Manager: **JACQUELINE** ZOPPI-TIGHE  Gaffer: **JOHN** BARKER

Props Master: **PAUL** DE CSERNATONY  Props Buyer: **TIM** YOUNGMAN

Art Director: **IAN** READE-HILL  Vision Mixer: **JOHN** BARCLAY

Engineering Manager: **ALAN** GODLEMAN  Camera Operator: **ANDY** MARTIN

Location Sound: **NIGEL** DAVIS  Sound Supervisor: **JEM** WHIPPEY  **Geoff** Moss

Editor: **MARK** WYBOURN  Script Supervisor: **GILLIAN** WOOD

First Assistant Director: **JULIE** SYKES  Visual Effects Designer: **JIM** FRANCIS

**Ed** Smith  **Mark** Howard  Digital Effects Designer: **CHRIS** VEALE

Make Up Designer: **ANDREA** FINCH  Costume Designer: **HOWARD** BURDEN

Line Producer: **JO** BENNETT  Production Designer: **MEL** BIBBY

Director of Photography: **PETER** MORGAN  Executive Producer: **DOUG** NAYLOR  Produced and Directed by: **ED** BYE

# INTRODUCTION
## ONLY THE GOOD...

'Only the Good ...' started out life entitled: 'Mirror, Mirror' then changed to 'Mirror/rorriM' then changed to 'Every Dog ...' before it finally arrived and stayed at 'Only the Good ...'

It was intended to be a two-parter, the second part being the unrecorded 'Earth' but the budget kiboshed that and forced us to make a one part cliff-hanger.

I don't really like cliff-hangers but it was the only solution.

The original assembly of the show lasted thirty-eight minutes and a whole sequence involving Rimmer meeting the crew's mirror universe opposites had to be dropped in the edit, including Craig playing, rather successfully, much to everyone's surprise, a Terry Thomas, ding-dong, type character. Craig is usually at his best playing characters very close to Lister but this time he really came good and it was a great shame the sequence had to be cut.

Some weeks after the final shoot day, I phoned Chris Barrie, concerned about the ending.

At this point, the ending left Rimmer semi-conscious on the floor, watching the antidote burn before his eyes after the vending machine had launched an 'Exocet' can of Coke at his head. The vending machine's final line was: '*Every Dog* ... has his day and today's the day and I'm the dog' and he then howled like a wolverine. The audience were left wondering how the hell Rimmer was going to get out of this one.

'Chris, we've shown the tape to a test audience and they're kind of upset by the ending.'

'It didn't test well?'

'It's too dark, according to the test audience. They want something more upbeat. I've got a new idea, I want you to come back for half a day.'

Chris readily agreed. The end hadn't worked for the test audience and he wanted to get it right.

And to this day, I think that's what Chris still believes. The truth, however, is something very different.

We'd finished the edit and a copy of the tape was lying around in my office at home, no sound effects, no model shots.

I hate people watching it in this state.

My two sons woke me up from a Sunday afternoon slumber.

'We've just watched the last show!' they said in unison.

'Oh, yeah?'

'Congratulations, Dad.'

'You like it?'

'... on making the worst, suckiest ending to any show ever.'

The youngest yelled: 'You've killed Rimmer, how could you kill Rimmer?'

'He's not in great shape, I admit it, but he's not dead. Not yet.'

'He's going to burn alive.'

'No, he isn't, it's a cliff-hanger. He's going to get out of it and save everyone.'

'But who's going to save him?'

'Ace Rimmer.' I said.

'Well, how are we supposed to know that?'

'You're not supposed to know that, that's why it's a cliff-hanger. You're supposed to watch it next time and find out.'

'It sucks.'

'It really sucks.'

'It sucks, big time.'

'Bigger than big time.'

What the hell do they know, I thought. One's twelve years old and never ties his shoe-laces and the other - well you should see the way he eats yoghurt. Chimpanzees can eat yoghurt better than him.

'What about the rest of it?' I asked.

They liked the rest of it. They really liked the rest of it. This made it even harder - out of the mouths of babes and sucklings and all that.

Now if there's one thing people who work in television absolutely hate, it's someone saying their wife or kids hated something about a show and as a consequence you should change it.

Years ago, I once got bollocked by a BBC executive for asking the people in the Wardrobe Department if they understood a particular one-liner Rob and I had written, which I felt was a little obscure.

The Wardobe people said they didn't get it, so we dropped it.

The Producer took me to one side: 'You shouldn't ask people in Wardobe what they think of the script, they make the costumes they're not qualified to pass judgement.'

'Yes, they are,' I said. 'They're people and people make up most of our audience.'

He wasn't for turning. 'It's your show, you get paid for writing the scripts. Don't be swayed by other people's opinions. Word will get round and everyone will think you don't know what you're doing.'

He walked off and missed my: 'But I don't.'

John Lloyd, on the other hand, (Producer of *Not the Nine O'clock News*, *Spitting Image*, and *Black Adder*) would ask everyone's opinion about everything, get huge amounts of feedback, collate it all, think about it, then make the final decision himself. I sided with Lloydy on this sort of thing.

Everyone on Red Dwarf, from cast to Tea Boy/Girl is encouraged to criticize the show.

If it makes the show better, I'll change anything.

I decided to re-shoot the ending.

I phoned Ed. 'I've played the last show to a test audience,' I said, 'and they hate the ending.'

'Your kids hate it, do they?'

'Not just my kids,' I said incredulously. 'I've played it to a couple of friends, the plumber's seen it, also the bloke who came to repair my video. That's a pretty fair representation of society.'

Ed played it to his test audience: Ruby, and their son, Max - he didn't know any plumbers he really trusted. They have the same reaction as Shoelace Boy and Look Out He's Eating Yoghurt.

We decided to re-shoot.

CAST & CREW CONFIDENTIAL

# RED DWARF VIII

'ONLY THE GOOD...'

### EPISODE 8

## Written by
## DOUG NAYLOR

© Grant Naylor Productions Limited 1998

# ONLY THE GOOD...

ONLY THE GOOD...

### TITLES

#### 1 MODEL SEQUENCE
Debris floats in space - the bones of a space freighter.

A pod powers out of the debris.

Typed on screen: 'Lone escape pod from SS *Hermes*, survivors one.'

Typing continues: 'Ship destroyed by cameleonic microbe...' This is deleted and retyped with 'Chamileionic mycrobe ...' This is also deleted and replaced with: 'By shape changing weird space thing. Non-essential electrics all down, including spell checker. Massage ends'

#### 2 MODEL SEQUENCE
Pod powers towards Red Dwarf.

#### 3 INT. LANDING BAY - DAY
Pod in landing bay.

Caption:- 6 hours later.

Pod starts to dissolve.

#### 4 INT. HOLLISTER'S QUARTERS - DAY
Hollister in bed is watching a crappy black and white movie on TV. A swamp beast carries a screaming woman out of a bog. Triple knock on door.

**HOLLISTER**
(Whispery hoarse) Come in.

Another triple knock.

**HOLLISTER**
(Whispery hoarse) Come in!!

Another triple knock.

**HOLLISTER**
(Whispery hoarse) Come in!!!!

Rimmer enters carrying a tray.

**RIMMER**
Can I come in, sir? I did knock, perhaps you didn't hear me. ~~How's your throat? Getting a little easier?~~

**HOLLISTER**
~~(Incomprehensible raspy swearing)~~

**RIMMER**
~~Oh, I am pleased to hear that, sir.~~ Your hot lemon, sir.

Hands him lemon drink. He drinks.

**HOLLISTER**
Goddamn yellow fever. I've still got that jowly, flabby puffiness around my cheeks.

**RIMMER**
Wasn't that there before your illness, sir? Yes, I'm sure it was because ... (Spots his look) ... let me tuck you in, sir.

**HOLLISTER**
How's life on probation, fouled it up yet?

**RIMMER**
Enjoying it, sir. Some directives for you to sign, sir.

Hands Hollister forms. He signs.

**HOLLISTER**
What's this Space Corps free pardon exonerating you of all crimes doing in here?

**RIMMER**
(Pretends to be shocked) Those people in Admin really need to pay more mind, sir. Honestly, tch. You can't rely on anyone these days, can you?

Hollister stares at him. He capitulates.

**RIMMER**
I'm so sorry, sir, it's just if I've got a record I'll never become an officer and command my own ship. And that's what I long for more than

---

Z  *Script cut from original broadcast.*

anything, sir - to be like you. Maybe thinner and in better condition and obviously without your clogged arteries, but that aside, sir, you're the person I admire the most.

**HOLLISTER**
Another ambition achieved.

**RIMMER**
You think I could become an officer, sir? One day, sir?

**Awkward pause.**

**HOLLISTER**
Thanks for the lemon drink, Rimmer. That'll be all.

**RIMMER**
You didn't answer my question, sir.

**HOLLISTER**
(Feigns losing voice - croaky groan)

**RIMMER**
You're just faking to avoid answering, aren't you, sir?

**HOLLISTER**
Look, it gives me no pleasure telling you this Rimmer, but I'm sorry - you're just not officer material.

**RIMMER**
Not officer material, sir?

**HOLLISTER**
A leader leads, he's not there for the fun of bossing people about.

**RIMMER**
(Stunned) Isn't he?

**HOLLISTER**
If you want to take my advice you'll redirect your energies and find something that you have got a genuine chance of succeeding at.

**RIMMER**
(Devastated) Like what, sir?

**HOLLISTER**
(Feigns losing voice again)

**RIMMER**
So you're saying I'm never going to become a captain, sir? Never?

**HOLLISTER**
(Feigns losing voice again)

**Talia, dressed in a black cloak-type outfit enters.**

**TALIA**
They said it was OK to drop by.

**HOLLISTER**
Talia? Well, hi.

**RIMMER**
Hi.

**HOLLISTER**
Rimmer was just leaving.

**TALIA**
(To Hollister) I can't believe we've run into one another again after all this time.

**HOLLISTER**
The Nanobots must have resurrected you too. You look wonderful.

**She holds his hand.**

**TALIA**
You made Captain, you've done so well. Your own ship - wow. I've got goose bumps.

**RIMMER**
The photograph of your wife, sir. Is it OK where it is, or should I turn it so it's facing the wall?

**HOLLISTER**
Dismiss, Rimmer.

**RIMMER**
Yes, sir. Thank you, sir. Nothing I can get you, ma'am? Tea, coffee, (Under his breath) ... packet of three?

## 5 INT. CORRIDOR - DAY

**Door opens. Rimmer slumps down the corridor. He stops at a dispensing machine.**

**RIMMER**
Me? Not make it. What does he know the big stupid yellow idiot.

**Rimmer takes out a coin with a bit of string on it and feeds it into the machine.**

**RIMMER**
He doesn't see my good side, my guile, my weasel cunning, when the going gets tough my ability to find good hiding places ...

**RIMMER**
He thinks I'm an imbecile. He really does. Heh! Me an imbecile!

**He gets his chocolate bar and then hauls up the coin.**

**MACHINE**
Alert, alert, a choccy nut bar, a choccy nut bar has been removed without payment, a choccy nut bar has been remoo ...

**RIMMER**
If you don't shut up I'll pour beef soup into your speaker and you'll drown.

**MACHINE**
(**Muffled**) Take your hand off my speaker then.

**LISTER**
Promise to shut up?

**MACHINE**
Promise.

**Rimmer removes hand. Pause.**

**Rimmer slams his hand over the speaker.**

**MACHINE**
(**Muffled**) ... without payment. Alert, alert, a choc ...

**RIMMER**
Shut up.

**MACHINE**
I shan't, alert, alert ...

**MACHINE**
Ha! I had my circuits crossed! ... alert, alert, chocolate abduction on Floor 341 -

**Rimmer sees trolley with masking tape on it. Grabs some and starts masking up speaker.**

**MACHINE**
(**Getting more and more muffled**) You'll not get away with this. I may not be able to see you but I know your taste in confectionery and I also, I also know, I also know, no, in fact, that's all I know,

just your taste in confectionery, but no matter, one day I'll hear your voice again and I'll expose you for the chocolate thieving dog you are.

**RIMMER**
I'm really scared. I'm being threatened by a dispensing machine.

**Hollister appears.**

**RIMMER**
What you going to do? Leave a horse's head made out of marzipan in my bed? (**Mimes biting nails and trembling**) Oh, Mummy, help, I'm really scared.

**HOLLISTER**
Rimmer, you forgot your tray.

**Rimmer takes tray while trying to hand muffle machine.**

**RIMMER**
Thank you, sir.

**MACHINE**
He stole some chocolate, he stole some ... (**Muffled**)

**Hollister retreats into quarters, warily.**

**MACHINE**
(**Muffled**) You are my nemesis. One day our paths will cross again. And I will destroy you.

**RIMMER**
And on that day I'll be the Captain of this ship.

## 6 INT. PRISON CORRIDOR – DAY

**Lister, Kryten and the Cat.**

**CAT**
It's OK for Mr Cushy, working for the Captain now. But what about me?  All that damned rock. My back's killing me, bud. Look at my spine? It's so curved, if you threw it away it'd come back. Rock, rock, rock, rock, rock, rock, rock. I ain't used to work and what job did they give me?

**KRYTEN**
Something to do with rock, sir?

**CAT**
Exactly. You know what they got me doing? I gotta put on all the rock albums on the PA system. I've gotta change those suckers once every forty-five minutes. I'm a physical wreck. Probation's killing me, buds.

**Cat makes a right, they go left.**

**LISTER**
What's that?

**KRYTEN**
Just a present to help cheer up Ms Kochanski.

**LISTER**
A calendar?

**KRYTEN**
A couple of days ago she was looking at the old calendar and she said it was the wrong time of the month, so I got her a new one.

**LISTER**
Uh, Kryten ...

**KRYTEN**
I'm going to tell her. The calendar people made a mistake, but let's leave this wrong month thing behind us. They were stupid, it was careless, but being grumpy and tearful about it is getting it way out of proportion.

**LISTER**
A little word in your audio receiver.

**Lister whispers to Kryten who listens astounded.**

**KRYTEN**
And this happens to all women? They become cranky and weird and yet you never see this in films or on TV? And men are supposed to be in control of the media? This is the biggest cover up since Watergate.

**LISTER**
Relax, it's not a big deal. I'll tell you what to do and how to behave, everything. Just trust me.

## 7 INT. KRYTEN AND KOCHANSKI'S QUARTERS - DAY.

**Kryten waits at the door for Kochanski. She enters.**

**KRYTEN**
Da da!!

**A banner is hanging across the cell. It says: 'Have a fantastic period'.**

**KRYTEN**
Thank goodness for Mr Lister. I nearly made such a fool of myself.

**Holds out a gift-wrapped tampon.**

**KRYTEN**
A little present, ma'am. All gift wrapped. I hope I chose the right size.

**KOCHANSKI**
(Charming, smiley, throughout) Dave told you to do this, didn't he?

**KRYTEN**
Isn't he wonderful?

**KOCHANSKI**
Oh yeah, sometimes he's so cute I could just eat him ...

**KRYTEN**
He explained everything to me, so I wouldn't embarrass myself. Come on then, open it. I want you to try it on. Maybe you could do a little twirl in it.

**KOCHANSKI**
Kryten, how can I put this ...?

**KRYTEN**
Is there something wrong, ma'am?

**It dawns.**

**KRYTEN**
He set me up, didn't he? This is absolutely not

what you're supposed to do when a woman is having a (**Points to banner**) ... Is the banner wrong too?

**Kochanski nods.**

**KRYTEN**
... he was lying. I've been duped by a master craftsman. Well two can play at this game.

**KOCHANSKI**
Oh yeah, what do you have in mind?

**KRYTEN**
Are you sure you have time for this, ma'am? I realize the next few days are very special for you. Don't you want to be playing tennis a lot in tight white jeans? I don't want to stop you from doing that and not forgetting all that blue stuff you've got to pour over things.

**KOCHANSKI**
Just tell me your plan for getting Dave back.

**KRYTEN**
Here's my idea.

**Kryten does mime.**

## 8 INT. RIMMER AND LISTER'S QUARTERS - EVENING.

**Rimmer and Lister are playing draughts.**

**LISTER**
That's Hol. He must want something.

**Holly materializes on screen.**

**HOLLY**
Thought you might like to hear some hot-off-the-press, confidential, insider information. There's going to be a cell inspection in about ten minutes. Keep it under your hat.

**Pops off screen. Guard sticks head round door.**

**GUARD**
Cell inspection in ten minutes.

**Holly back on screen.**

**HOLLY**
Told you.

**LISTER**
Thanks, Hol, that was most helpful.

**HOLLY**
When it comes to being ahead of the game,
I'm the man.

**RIMMER**
If you don't mind me asking - where did you get
that priceless nugget of information way before it
got into the public domain?

**HOLLY**
I've hacked into the ship's computer system, got
into the prison log. I've also managed to get a
goosey at the supplies inventory. I've discovered
stuff in there that'll make your hair stand on end.

**LISTER**
What stuff?

**HOLLY**
Brylcreem it's called. Put it on your head and it
makes your hair stand on end. Apparently, we've
only got two jars left, so if you need some, let me
know. As soon as I've got anything else that'll be
useful, I'll be back.

**RIMMER**
See you in about twenty-five years then.

**Holly laughs sarcastically.**

**LISTER**
This little scar's itchy today. It must be all
the dust.

**RIMMER**
You've got a scar, when did you get that?

**LISTER**
You know those complimentary pens the hospital
guys were handing out? You know, 'most
accidents happen in the home, so be careful'
ones. I accidentally stabbed myself in the head
with one.

**RIMMER**
Where were you?

**LISTER**
Oh, I wasn't at home so I didn't feel stupid
or anything.

**RIMMER**
That's not a scar. That's a nick. That is a scar.

**LISTER**
(Squints) Where'd you get that?

**RIMMER**
From a fight, years ago. Duel.

**LISTER**
A duel? You? Get out of town.

**RIMMER**
Not a duel, *Duel*: the old Steven Spielberg movie.
A friend of mine attacked me with the video case.
Some stupid argument about who had the
coolest bicycle clips. I got him back though. I
peed in his Mum's steam iron, he had yellow T-
shirts for a week.

**The alarm clock goes off. Rimmer goes to turn
it off.**

**RIMMER**
Why's that going off?

**Rimmer takes a note stuck to the clock.**

**RIMMER**
It's from Kryten. 'Look under the draught board.'

**LISTER**
Another note. 'Dear Mr Lister, thanks for your
wonderful advice regarding Ms Kochanski. In
return, I thought I'd steal Baxter's stash of illegal
hootch and hide it in your shower. I am laughing
as I write this, knowing your cell is about to be
searched and imagining the panic now gripping
your soul.'

**RIMMER**
My God.

**LISTER**
Oh God!

**RIMMER**
What the hell are we going to do? We've got an
inspection in five minutes.
WE'RE ON PROBATION!

**LISTER**
Down the loo, down the sink.

**They start pouring the bottles down loo and basin.**

**RIMMER**
Baxter's going to kill us if he finds out we're doing this.

**LISTER**
The Captain's going to kill us if we don't.

**RIMMER**
But Baxter? You've seen what he's like? Grizzly bears run screaming from him. Last week he was playing poker, ran out of money, he bet his right nut on a pair of jacks. A pair of jacks? That's how hard he is.

**A red light starts flashing above the loo: 'Tank full.'**

**LISTER**
Smeg! The tank's full.

**RIMMER**
What we going to do? We've still got two bottles left.

**LISTER**
We're going to have to drink it.

**RIMMER**
Drink it? This is Baxter's hootch. It's about 300% proof. A bottle of this would get the entire Greek Navy drunk.

**LISTER**
It'll put hairs on your chest.

**RIMMER**
It'll put hairs on your lips. It'll put hairs on your hairs. It's lethal.

**LISTER**
You want to get caught in possession of illegal hootch? Get drinking.

**RIMMER**
Have we got any mixers?

**LISTER**
You are wetter than a driving instructor's handshake, aren't you? Get it down your gob.

**Lister throws him a bottle and starts drinking the other one.**

Lister tries to hide how potent it is.

**RIMMER**
What's it like?

**LISTER**
(Hoarse) It's OK.

**Rimmer drinks and starts to shake uncontrollably.**

## 9 BLACK/BLANK SCREEN (TIME CUT)

**Caption: '5 minutes sshhlater ...'**

## 10 INT. PRISON QUARTERS – DAY

**Ackerman enters.**

**ACKERMAN**
Inspection.

**Lister and Rimmer sit, swaying slightly.**

**ACKERMAN**
On your feet.

They rise unsteadily and make their way to their beds, holding onto the furniture.

**ACKERMAN**
Stand by your bunks.

Ackerman looks at them suspiciously and sniffs bottles.

**ACKERMAN**
You're drunk!

**LISTER**
Drunk, sir? No, sir.

**RIMMER**
Absolutely not, sir. No, no, no, no.

Ackerman looks at them trying to decide.

**ACKERMAN**
Who fancies a kebab?

**LISTER/RIMMER**
Oh, yeah. Brilliant. Yeah, great.

**LISTER**
Smeg, he's tricked us.

Rimmer goes poker stiff and collapses.

**LISTER**
It must have been the sherry trifle at lunch, sir. Told him not to go back for seconds. Sir.

Lister falls asleep on Ackerman's shoulder.

**ACKERMAN**
Call the Medi-bay. We need two stomach pumps, 'super suck.'

## 11 INT. CANTEEN - FOLLOWING MORNING.
Kochanski, Cat, Kryten eating.

**KOCHANSKI**
It's Baxter.

Baxter walks over with friends.

**BAXTER**
Your two mates skulled my hootch.
When they get out of hospital and there's no guards about, this is what's going to happen to them.

Baxter picks up rolls off Cat's plate and squeezes them into nothing.

**CAT**
You're going to squeeze their rolls? That's irritating but, hey, in many ways they'll be quite relieved.

Baxter leaves.

**KRYTEN**
What have I done?

## 12 INT. MEDI-BAY - DAY.
Lister and Rimmer in beds.

**RIMMER**
Wuggghhhh.

**LISTER**
Ugggghhhh

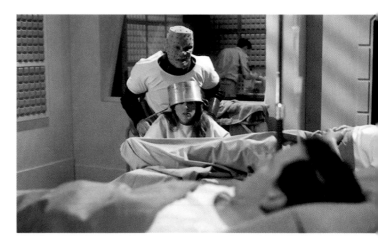

Kryten and Kochanski enter. Kryten has blue spots on his face and he's pushing Kochanski in a wheelchair with a saucepan on her head.

**KOCHANSKI**
Baxter's out to mash you. You've got to escape. We all have.

**KRYTEN**
Security's lax here. If we can make it to the Landing Bay, steal a ship and Bob's your Skutter.

**RIMMER**
Where's the Cat?

**KRYTEN**
He should be getting himself hospitalized any second.

### 13 INT. CANTEEN - LUNCH

**Guards watching. Cat squeezes in between prisoners and sits next to Big Meat.**

**CAT**
Pass the salt, would you?

**As Big Meat passes salt, Cat steals a load of his fries.**

**Big Meat stares at him.**

**CAT**
(**Mouthful**) That guy there took some of your fries.

**As Big Meat turns the Cat steals more fries.**

**BIG MEAT**
What the hell are you doing, Shirley?

**CAT**
I'm stealing your fries ... Fat boy. (**Cat eats Baxter's food**) Mmmmmm, this is good. Tasty!

**BIG MEAT**
There ain't no-one more bad-ass, evil than me in the whole of hell. What makes you think you can diss me and live?

**CAT**
Cos things are changing round here. From now on, marshmallow ass, you're my bitch.

**Cat thrusts his head forward so he can get hit.**

**BIG MEAT**
Your what?

**CAT**
B-I- (**He's not sure of the spelling**) ... itch - bitch. That's what you look like, that's what you are.

Understand?

**BIG MEAT**
(**Pause then**) OK.

**CAT**
What?

**BIG MEAT**
Anyone tough-talks me gotta be a no-lobbing pug. You want me to be your bitch, that's fine by me, sir.

**CAT**
You sure you don't want to just hit me a couple of times, test me out.

**BIG MEAT**
No, sir. I'm your bitch. From now on I'm your jiggly-wiggly, roll-over, sweet patooie, honey bun, missy. I just wanna make you happy.

**CAT**
Then hit me.

**BIG MEAT**
And hurt my baby's kisser? Nothing doing.

**CAT**
Damn.

## 14 INT. MEDI-BAY - DAY.

**The four in bed. Two nurses are checking pulses. Lister's eyes widen as he realizes one of them is the Cat. Cat grins. Nurse 2 exits.**

**CAT**
We can't hang around, we've gotta be out of here by five o'clock.

**LISTER**
What's so special about five o'clock?

**CAT**
Five o'clock's bed-bath time and apparently I'm doing 'em.

## 15 INT. LANDING BAY - DAY.

**The posse emerge from a grill then creep along. Suddenly they come to an area which has been eaten away, as if by acid.**

**KRYTEN**
The microbe which destroyed the Hermes. It's on Red Dwarf.

**LISTER**
How?

**RIMMER**
The microbe's chameleonic. So, it must have been the escape pod the one Talia whatsher-name arrived on.

**LISTER**
We've got to go back and tell them.

**RIMMER**
What about our escape?

**LISTER**
It could be days before they discover this. If we go back now they've got a chance to work on an antidote.

**RIMMER**
You're just acting all brave and manly to impress her, aren't you?

**KOCHANSKI**
No, Dave's right. He's looking at the big picture.

**RIMMER**
Yes, the big picture involves you, no clothes and a hay stack.

## 16 INT. CANARY AREA - DAY

**Hollister addresses prisoners.**

**HOLLISTER**
Red Dwarf is being devoured from within by a corrosive micro-organism.

**RIMMER**
Yes, it's called lust.

**HOLLISTER**
In two weeks there'll be nothing left of the ship but a dead carcass.

**RIMMER**
Same as Lister if I get hold of him.

**HOLLISTER**
As you probably know we don't have enough craft for everyone to be rescued. So most of you will be staying behind to die. Oh, there's an apology about that in the internal mail. The following names have been selected at random from the prisoner roll call to join us in the rescue craft. Brown.

**Brown goes berserk.**

**HOLLISTER**
... Polsen.

**Polsen goes berserk.**

**HOLLISTER**
... Lister.

**Lister goes berserk.**

**HOLLISTER**
... that's it.

**RIMMER**
That's it?

**HOLLISTER**
I'm sorry, that's all we have room for.

**RIMMER**
We could have escaped. Now look at us. If we'd done the right thing, and taken the cowhearted, weasel option we'd be circling the rotting Dwarf right now making faces at this lot through the port holes.

**LISTER**
Sir, I don't want to go. I want to give my place to

~~Baxter looms behind him.~~

**LISTER**
Baxter. Because it's the least I can do.

**BAXTER**
We're square now.

~~Baxter walks off to the rescue craft.~~

## 17 EXT. CGI/MODEL SEQUENCE
**Blue Midgets and Starbugs leaving Red Dwarf.**

## 18 INT. PIPEY AREA - DAY
**The posse examine an area destroyed by the organism. Kryten has captured some in a glass tube.**

**KRYTEN**
Just as I suspected. Created in a lab and programed not to destroy glass.

**CAT**
So all we need is a plutonium-powered green house and we're home free.

**KRYTEN**
We need an antidote. Something that can neutralize the corrosive negativity of the microbe.

**LISTER**
Something with a corrosive positivity.

**CAT**
So, where'd we get that?

**HOLLY**
There's nothing in *Yellow Pages*.

**KOCHANSKI**
A mirror universe. A universe where things are diametrically opposite to this one. There negative becomes positive, and a virus becomes an antidote.

~~RIMMER~~
A mirror universe, where everything's the opposite.

**HOLLY**
Politicians will be trusted, children'll love sprouts and Rap music will be really good.

**CAT**
How do we get to this mirror universe?

**RIMMER**
You mean because we've got no form of transport apart from my old bike? Can't Krytie stick some sort of gizmo to one of the wheels so it can cross dimensions when it's going down hill really fast?

**KOCHANSKI**
You're not helping.

**RIMMER**
That's not my job.

**KRYTEN**
Sir. We now have the run of the ship. Access to all the technology on board. Creating a temporary ~~portal could be possible.~~

## 19 INT. HOLLISTER'S QUARTERS - DAY.
**A large glass prism is connected to some gizmo which points towards a long mirror which turns the mirror into a whirly, watery substance that swirls about.**

**KRYTEN**
If there's even the slightest imperfection in the prism, the mirror universe may be an imperfect version of our own. That's something we won't know until we get there.

**Rimmer takes the virus tube and enters the mirror, as he passes through it the machine fuses and blows up.**

**KRYTEN**
It's overloaded. We've lost Mr Rimmer.

**CAT**
At last - things are looking up.

**LISTER**
How long is it going to take to fix that thing?

**KRYTEN**
Best guess: about twenty minutes.

## 20 INT. FLIPPED HOLLISTER'S QUARTERS - DAY

The whole picture is flipped. Rimmer walks out of the mirror, realizes he can't get back.

**RIMMER**
~~My scar's swapped sides.~~

On TV the swamp thing movie. Although in this version the woman is carrying a screaming swamp thing.

Triple knock on the door. Rimmer gets into bed. Another triple knock. Hollister enters carrying a tray. He executes a Rimmer salute.

**HOLLISTER**
Can I come in, sir? I did knock, perhaps you didn't hear me. ~~How's your throat? Getting a little easier?~~

**RIMMER**
~~(Squeaks with excitement)~~

**HOLLISTER**
Here's your hot lemon, sir.

**Takes lemon.**

**RIMMER**
Thank you, uh, (**Reads his stripes**) Private Nobody. ~~So, how's life on ... probation? Fouled it up yet?~~

**HOLLISTER**
~~Enjoying it, sir.~~

**Hollister hands him papers.**

**HOLLISTER**
Oh, er ... a few directives to sign, sir.

**RIMMER**
(**Warming to his task**) Of course, laddie.

**RIMMER**
A free pardon exonerating you from all crimes?

**He takes out the free pardon one, balls it up and tosses it into the bin.**

**HOLLISTER**
(**Pretending to be shocked**) I don't know how that got in there, sir. I, uh ...

**RIMMER**
(**Smiling**) Want to be an officer, don't you, laddie?

**HOLLISTER**
Oh, sir, could I? One day, could I be ...?

**RIMMER**
(**Smiling**) No, I don't think you could.

**Rimmer starts to sign the forms but scrawls something incredibly babyish until he swaps hands and signs effortlessly.**

**RIMMER**
Of course, it's a mirror universe. Everything's opposite.

**Rimmer lifts up the bed sheet and looks down the front of his trousers.**

**RIMMER**
~~Boa constrictor! (To Hollister) Quick, get me a gun. (Realizes) No, wait.~~ My God. This is going to take some getting used to. ~~I'll need some sort~~ of anti-gravity harness ~~carting~~ that lot around ~~all day.~~

**Talia enters, dressed in black, in a chinese-type, two-piece suit.**

**TALIA**
They said it was OK to drop by. You look wonderful.

**RIMMER**
So do you. (**To Hollister**) That'll be all, Shambles.

**HOLLISTER**
Yes, sir. (**He exits**)

**She holds his hand.**

**TALIA**
You made Captain, you've done so well.
Your own ship - wow. I've got goose bumps.

**RIMMER**
So have I.

**TALIA**
Let me kiss you.

**She leans forward. Rimmer grabs her and kisses her passionately.**

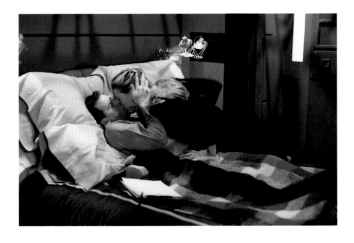

**TALIA**
What are you doing!?

**RIMMER**
(**Grinning**) I'm giving you a big wet snog with oodles of Tommy Tongue.

**TALIA**
But I'm your sister.

**RIMMER**
(**Pause**) Yes, of course. But, uh, I, uh, I was really pleased to see you. And uh ...

**TALIA**
You French kissed me!

**RIMMER**
No, it was nearer Antwerp, I Belgium kissed you. I've been really ill and uh ... You're the Captain's sister ...?

**Rimmer pretends to faint. Then wakes up.**

**RIMMER**
Oh my God, what a terrible dream. (**Pretends to notice her for the first time**) Oh, hi, Sis, it's me Arnie, your bro.

**He grabs her nose and gives it a twist, then shakes her head about from side to side.**

**RIMMER**
Get your big old lumpy bum down here and give us a big hug.

**TALIA**
Capt. Rimmer I'm Sister Talia Garret, your personal spiritual adviser.

**Talia starts to exit.**

**RIMMER**
Sis, sister! Whoever you are - oh smeg.

## 21 INT. SCIENCE DEPARTMENT - DAY

A woman, blonde, is doing some secretarial work.

**RIMMER**
Excuse me.

**SECRETARY KOCHANSKI**
Yes?

**RIMMER**
I wonder, could you tell me what this is?

**SECRETARY KOCHANSKI**
You'll need to ask the professor then. He does all that stupid sciency brain-box-type stuff.

Professor Cat enters.

**PROFESSOR CAT**
Somebody call?

**RIMMER**
Professor?

**PROFESSOR CAT**
Yes, Captain.

**RIMMER**
Perhaps you could help me. What's this?

Professor Cat examines it.

**PROFESSOR CAT**
It's an alkali.

**RIMMER**
Oh yes, what's it called?

**PROFESSOR CAT**
Cesiumfrancolithic myxialobidiumrixydixydox-hidexidroxhide. You look surprised?

**RIMMER**
I never thought I'd ever hear you say that. Can you write it down for me?

**PROFESSOR CAT**
Certainly, can I have an extremely long piece of paper, my dear.

## 22 INT. FLIPPED CORRIDOR - DAY.

Rimmer runs down corridor with his formula.

**RIMMER**
The antidote. I did it.

## 23 INT. HOLLISTER'S QUARTERS - DAY

Rimmer steps through the mirror. The ship is in the middle of a ship quake. Everthing's dissolving.

**RIMMER**
I did it.

## 24 INT. CORRIDOR - DAY

Rimmer dashes into the corridor. Everything's dissolving there too.

**RIMMER**
Whu-where is everyone?

**MACHINE**
They've repaired the machine and crossed into the mirror universe. You're the highest rank crew member left on the ship, so I suppose that makes you Captain. Congratulations Capt.

**RIMMER**
Smeg off.

**Rimmer runs back into -**

## 25 INT. HOLLISTER'S QUARTERS - DAY

**Rimmer runs back towards the mirror. It is now back to normal. Rimmer turns and looks at the machine. The microbe has landed on it and the machine has half dissolved. He looks at the paper.**

## 26 INT. CORRIDOR - DAY.

**Rimmer runs down corridor, turns camera left and starts running towards lab.**

**MACHINE**
Where you going?

**RIMMER**
To make up the formula.

**MACHINE**
I think you'll find that the formula on that piece of paper has now turned into the formula for the virus because you've left the mirror universe, so

it's turned back into its opposite. Ha,ha,ha.

**Rimmer looks at paper. Close up.**

**RIMMER**
Smeg, you're right. This is a disaster.

**MACHINE**
No, there could still be a happy ending.

**RIMMER**
How?

**MACHINE**
Remember that chocolate bar you still owe me for - you could always pay me back before you snuff it.

**RIMMER**
How's that a happy ending?

**MACHINE**
Well, it's a happy ending for me. At least my totals will tally.

**RIMMER**
Why don't you smegging well smeg off you annoying little smeggy smegging smegger.

**Rimmer runs off down the corridor.**

**MACHINE**
Every dog has his day and today's the day ...

**A can of Coke screams down the corridor after Rimmer. Coke can hits Rimmer in the head and he falls face first into the floor.**

**MACHINE**
... and I'm the dog.

**He lies there watching the 'antidote' burn.**

**RIMMER**
Smeg.

**A sandalled foot stamps on the flaming 'antidote'. Rimmer looks up to see death standing before him.**

**DEATH**
Arnold Judas Rimmer. Your life is over. Come with me ...

**He helps Rimmer to his feet.**

**DEATH**
... We will travel to the River Styx, where you will place a coin in the mou ...

**RIMMER**
Not today, matey.

**Rimmer knees Death in the balls. SFX as they clank together. Death doubles over.**

**RIMMER**
Remember, only the good die young.

**Rimmer legs it.**

**DEATH**
That's never happened before ...

**Death falls into a crumpled heap on the floor.**

## 27  BLACK/BLANK  SCREEN
**Caption - 'The end'.**

**Then that disappears and there is a long pause before a second caption appears, which says:**

**'The smeg it is'.**

## TITLES

# ONLY THE GOOD...

ONLY THE GOOD...

## *Cast & Crew*

Written by: **DOUG** NAYLOR

Rimmer: **CHRIS** BARRIE  Lister: **CRAIG** CHARLES  Cat: **DANNY** JOHN-JULES

Kryten: **ROBERT** LLEWELLYN  Kochanski: **CHLOË** ANNETT  Holly: **NORMAN** LOVETT

Hollister: **MAC** McDONALD  Ackerman: **GRAHAM** McTAVISH  Talia: **HEIDI** MONSEN

Dispensing Machine: **TONY** SLATTERY  Baxter: **RICKY** GROVER  Big Meat: **DAVID** VERREY

Grim Reaper: **ED** BYE


Casting Director: **LINDA** GLOVER  Music: **HOWARD** GOODALL

Production Accountant: **MIKE** AMOS  Graphic Designer: **ANDY** SPENCE

General Manager GNP LTD: **HELEN** NORMAN  Location Manager: **KEN** HAWKINS

Production Co-ordinator: **RACHEL** STEWART

Post-Production Co-ordinator: **SIMON** BURCHELL

Stage Manager: **JACQUELINE** ZOPPI-TIGHE  Production Team: **KELLY** SPARKS

**JACKIE** KELLY  **LUCY** GOSSAGE  **LUCY** TULLET  **GINA** HINTON  Gaffer: **JOHN** BARKER

Props: **PAUL** DE CSERNATONY  **NEIL** DAVIES  **MICHALA** JERMY  **NIGEL** PINHAY

Props Buyer: **TIM** YOUNGMAN  Art Director: **IAN** READE-HILL

Vision Mixer: **JOHN** BARCLAY  Engineering Manager: **ALAN** GODLEMAN

Camera Operator: **ANDY** MARTIN  Location Sound: **NIGEL** DAVIS

Boom Operator: **MIKE** REARDON  Post-Production Sound: **JEM** WHIPPEY  **Geoff** Moss  Editor: **MARK** WYBOURN  Script Associate: **PAUL** ALEXANDER

Script Supervisor: **GILLIAN** WOOD  First Assistant Director: **JULIE** SYKES

Visual Effects Designer: **JIM** FRANCIS  **Ed** Smith  **Mark** Howard

Digital Effects Designer: **CHRIS** VEALE  Make Up Designer: **ANDREA** FINCH

**Christine** Allsopp  **Sarah** Berry  Costume Designer: **HOWARD** BURDEN  **Gill** Shaw  **Richard** Sale

Line Producer: **JO** BENNETT  Production Designer: **MEL** BIBBY

Director of Photography: **PETER** MORGAN  Executive Producer: **DOUG** NAYLOR

Produced and Directed by: **ED** BYE

# OUTRO
## ONLY THE GOOD...

**F**or the re-shoot, I'd decided Ace Rimmer was going to save the day.

As I drove to the location I had another idea. What if we illustrate Rimmer's metaphoric struggle to regain consciousness by having Death appear, bit of chit chat, ending with Rimmer kneeing him in the balls and legging it.

I told Ed I knew we were about to shoot in ten minutes and Chris Barrie was already in his Ace Rimmer's wig but I had another idea and I wanted him to choose which one was better. I outlined the idea.

Ed listened: 'So you're suggesting we throw away the original script and get someone in to play Death?'

'Right.'

'And we're going to shoot this in the next nine minutes.'

'Right.'

'What's Death going to look like?'

'Like in an Ingmar Bergman movie, a big black cloak and a scythe. Surely we can get a big black cloak and a scythe in the next eight minutes, somehow.'

'And who's going to play the part of Death?'

I was ready for that question. 'Remember that bloke we used for the demented Dalek voice-over in the Anniversary Special? He was good. In fact, he was damn good and I hear he's available and actually in Shepperton Studios this very morning. Plus he's cheap. We'll be able to get him for free.'

'You mean me?' Ed said, seeing it coming a mile off. Pause. 'OK.'

Not many Directors will work like this. Chucking out the script seconds before you're about to shoot because a better idea comes along, find a costume and a prop at a second's notice, and then play the part and direct himself.

Thankfully, Ed doesn't have any problems working like this, providing it makes the show funnier.

He then suggested the: 'That's never happened to me before' line and went haring off in search of a black cloak and scythe.

Half way to the door he stopped: 'Do me a favour, don't think of any more ideas, OK?' A pause. 'Unless they're funnier.'

'OK.' I agreed.

And then he disappeared, returning five minutes later with a large piece of black cyc cloth used for model shoots, a pair of sandals - found in the boot of someone's car and a scythe.

He'd made it look so easy.

It made me want to think of another idea just to see if he could get the props in time. 'Wait,' I wanted to cry: 'I've got a new idea. Forget Death - Rimmer's saved by a tap-dancing walrus dressed like a 19th-century Bolivian General carrying an unnaturally large stick of celery.'

He'd probably have got that together in time too.

Finally, to everyone who worked on Red Dwarf, past and present, my undying thanks. It was a privilege to be there.

Best wishes,

Doug Naylor.

## RED DWARF SERIES VIII VIDEOS

### BYTE 1 – BACK IN THE RED
Red Dwarf is back in style with the first four episodes from Series VIII, together with a selection of Red Dwarf VIII Smeg Ups.

Back In The Red – Part 1
Not only have the Nanobots re-created Red Dwarf, they've also populated the ship with its original crew. This is extremely good news for Rimmer.

Back In The Red – Part 2
Rimmer is invited to dinner with the Captain and, to make the evening go with a swing, he douses himself with the Sexual Magnetism Virus, making him irresistible to the female crew.

Back In The Red – Part 3
The Dwarfers face two years in the brig for crimes against the Space Corps. Realising their defence has more holes than Lister's underpants, they escape to prove their innocence.

Cassandra
Taking Holly's advice, Lister joins the Canaries – a battle-hardened convict army trained to go on suicide missions, and not, as he thought, the prison choir!

Starring Chris Barrie, Craig Charles, Danny John-Jules, Robert Llewellyn, Norman Lovett and Chloë Annett.
Written by Doug Naylor
Produced and Directed by Ed Bye
Executive Producer: Doug Naylor

### BYTE 2 – KRYTIE TV
The four remaining episodes from Series VIII, a second batch of Smeg Ups and a Red Dwarf parody of the *Star Wars* trailer.

Krytie TV
Kryten starts his own pirate TV station to entertain the prisoners.
Written by Doug Naylor & Paul Alexander

Pete – Part 1
When Rimmer and Lister are forced to take on the guards in a basketball game, they sabotage the opposition's half-time juice with 'Boing' – the virility enhancement drug.
Written by Doug Naylor

Pete – Part 2
The Dwarfers discover birds are descended from dinosaurs when they de-evolve a sparrow into a T-Rex!
Written by Doug Naylor & Paul Alexander

Only The Good . . .
Rimmer crosses into a mirror universe where he discovers another version of himself captaining the ship.
Written by Doug Naylor

Starring Chris Barrie, Craig Charles, Danny John-Jules, Robert Llewellyn, Norman Lovett and Chloë Annett.
Produced and Directed by Ed Bye
Executive Producer: Doug Naylor

Visit the Red Dwarf website: www.reddwarf.co.uk